Is This
MyStory?

Helping young people develop
Confidence, Courage, Creativity and Compassion
through the magic of narrative.

Nicole Feledy

Is This MyStory - Helping Young People Develop Confidence, Courage, Creativity and Compassion Through the Magic of Narrative.

Author: © Nicole Feledy

National Library of Australia Cataloguing-in-Publication entry

Author:	Feledy, Nicole.
Title:	Is this my story? : take control and be the author of your own life rather than a character in someone else's / Nicole Feledy.
ISBN:	9780987277206 (pbk.)
Subjects:	Self-actualization (Psychology)
	Life skills.
	Quality of life.
	Youth--Life skills guides.
	Youth--Conduct of life Dewey Number: 158.1

Published by This Is My Time Pty Ltd ABN 31141165068
Gold Coast Australia

Editing: Clear Communications: www.clearcommunications.net.au

Designed and printed with www.loveofbooks.com.au

For orders and further information about Is This MyStory courses and seminars

Website: www.isthismystory.com

Email: nicole@isthismystory.com

A Map to the Door
of Lifelong Learning

Acknowledgements

Although the experience of writing may be solitary, the path of a writer is not. To say I have been extremely fortunate in my quest to become an author would be an understatement. I have been blessed by supportive colleagues, caring friends and a loving family. So,

To every student I have had the privilege to teach,

To those in the English staffroom,

To Nick whose courage in the face of adversity continues to inspire,

To Asha who breathes confidence,

To Dave who encourages creativity,

To Kez whose compassion knows no bounds,

To Denis & Denise who gave so much more than life,

To Talan & Willow who demonstrate patience and awareness beyond their years,

To Danny whose intelligent wisdom, forthright perspective and enduring love kept me challenged and focused and without whom this book would never have been written.

Thank you.
You are my shining,
spiralling lights.

Disclaimer

All of the information contained within this book is general. The intent is to offer generalised comments only and is not to be used as a recommendation for any particular individual. All characters are fictional and any resemblance to a person is purely coincidental.

This book is sold with the understanding that the author is an English teacher. While every care has been taken in researching and compiling this book, the information is not intended to replace professional advice. The book is not a counselling tool, nor does it offer answers to psychological, legal or any other problems. Therefore, if you wish to apply ideas contained in this book, you are taking full responsibility for your actions.

The author and publisher disclaim any warranties (express or implied), merchantability, or fitness for any particular purpose. The author and publisher shall in no event be held liable to any party for any direct, indirect, punitive, special, incidental or other consequential damages arising directly or indirectly from any use of this material, which is provided 'as is', and without warranties.

The author and publisher do not warrant the performance, effectiveness or applicability of any sites listed or linked to in this book. All links are for information purposes only and are not warranted for content, accuracy or any other implied or explicit purpose.

Two roads diverged in a wood, and I –

I took the one less travelled by,

and that has made all the difference.

—Robert Frost

Contents

Chapter 3: The Stage:

Chapter 4: The Audience:

Foreword

Qualifications, Certifications and Credibility

Over the past 14 years I have taught and encouraged many students from a variety of backgrounds. I have studied educational psychology, but I am not a psychologist. I have studied student welfare but I am not a counsellor. I have studied Neuro-linguistic programming (NLP) but I am not a master practitioner. I am a teacher, a listener, a learner and a writer; and I am proud to be so.

However, this was not always the case. My wake-up call occurred a few years ago when an acquaintance called me to account for saying I was 'just a teacher'. He questioned why I diminished the importance of what I did by describing myself as *just* a teacher. He suggested that the use of the word 'just' implied I did not value what I did or who I was.

Wondering if he was right, I explored the thought patterns underpinning the 'just a teacher' statement. What began to emerge was a restrictive belief system; a belief system that had bound me to repetitive patterns and limited my performance.

I realised that I had been holding on to a belief that a psychology degree was more valid than a teaching one. I had believed that a degree in psychology or counselling endowed the holder with a credibility that I could not hope to match. Maybe, implicit in the 'just a teacher' statement was a feeling of inferiority and frustration. Certainly the belief that I was 'not qualified' had inhibited me. I used it as an excuse not to start my own business. It even stunted my writing. I had reconciled to waiting until after

1

my children finished school to return to university and study psychology to qualify for the work I thought I wanted to do.

But then I stopped. I stopped playing the 'when I have x I can do y' game and began to focus on *my* skills and *my* talents rather than the skills and talents of others. I realised that the role of a teacher is frequently misunderstood. Teachers are often viewed as 'disseminators of knowledge' or 'purveyors of skills'. Yet they have so much more to offer.

Teachers are in a unique position to view young people in their 'natural habitat'. They watch as children grow from innocent naivety, through gangly teenage awkwardness to mature young adult awareness and they notice the patterns that occur time and time again. Teachers see what 'works' and what doesn't; they observe how some young people seem imbued with the skills and attitudes to cope with life's challenges and they see the many more who are in need of extra support and guidance.

I realised all I really wanted to do was teach. However, I wanted to teach more than English. I wanted to teach students what they could *do* with what they were learning, and more importantly I wanted to teach them *how* to learn. I wanted to support them as they developed and expanded their awareness through the books they read, the stories they heard and the ideas they shared. I wanted to help teenagers realise, the more self-aware they are, the more they can shape their future. I wanted to encourage teenagers to live *their* lives. I realised I wanted to *be* a teacher and that I did have the qualifications and experience necessary to be a teacher.

So I deliberately stepped away from my old repetitive and restrictive belief systems and, began to write. I drew confidence from my knowledge, practice and skills. I called upon my own resources.

However, by my side were all of the students I have had the privilege to teach. While writing I recalled their courage and determination. I remembered the moments when the veil lifted and they accepted responsibility for their own learning. In that instant they understood that they held the power to choose their own destiny. I know that my students have taught me as much as I could ever teach them. They were the inspiration for *MyStory*.

Nicole Feledy

The World of Expression

In a world of uncertainty and doubt, fear leads us. We seek safety by searching for acceptance, reassurance and affirmation. Instead, we find conditions, boundaries, restrictions and penalties and so we compromise, we tolerate, we endure.

Yet ...

In a world of belief and faith, love guides us. We use understanding and optimism to inspire awareness and trust. We find confidence and loyalty and share comprehension, compassion and faithfulness.

Would you like to live in a world of belief and faith?

First, suspend disbelief.
Be open to possibility and creativity.
Then ask yourself: What is my 'story'?

Let me support you on your quest. Use the scaffold I provide in this book as a map to the door of lifelong learning. Discover the confidence within. Accept responsibility for yourself. Choose to write your *MyStory*.

Begin with the end in mind.

Reflect

What do you want to achieve by reading this book?

_____
_____
_____

MyStory *is an unusual book in that it combines short stories with theory and theory with practice. So, read the narratives, they support the ideas you are exploring. Sometimes the narrative serves as a warm-up, preparing you for the ideas you are about to encounter. Other times the stories consolidate what you have already read.*

This first story offers a taste of what is to come ...

Story: The Key

The key was old and ornate. Engraved on its shaft was a series of four, interlocked, spiralling circles.

John turned a shy gaze towards Liz. 'Are you ready?'

She smiled. Her response was carefully measured and resolute. 'Yes.'

It was a smile that gave confidence. The sort of smile which could only be shared between friends, friends who had settled into a comfortable pattern of acceptance and understanding. Of course there had been those awkward moments between the ages of 12 and 14, where an undefined relationship and shifting sense of identity had caused confusion and discomfort. However, that passed as awkward adolescence gave way to a more relaxed sense of self.

So, to say John and Liz were 'just friends' understated the awareness they shared. Although neither felt any romantic inclination towards the other, theirs was a relationship built on loyalty, trust and love. Neither felt jealous while the other soared the dizzy heights of first love. Instead they waited to offer support or illuminate some mystery about the opposite sex. And when love fizzled, they were on call to nurse the broken heart.

They looked nothing alike. However as 'opposites', they seemed to form a natural Yin Yang symbol. Liz's long dark locks were the perfect foil for the sun bleached mop gracing John's head. Whereas Liz retained a perfectly groomed appearance, John wore a wildness that refused to be tamed. Perhaps it was the perpetually long fringe that fell in waves across sea green eyes. Or maybe it was the loose fashion sense featuring clothes wrestled straight off hell's floordrobe. In either case, John radiated restlessness. Liz on the other hand was pocket-sized. Fine elfin features housed eyes so dark they mirrored night. Although inquisitive by nature, Liz was patient; her tranquil manner as refined as John's was rough. Yet somehow, when they were together, they enhanced each other's strengths and diluted each other's weaknesses. They shared their courage, they gave each other compassion, they offered each other confidence and they encouraged each other's creativity.

John's strong arm looped around Liz's shoulders, this was a moment they had been planning for weeks. Even though neither could recall whose idea it was initially, both agreed using the key was the perfect way to celebrate the start of their final year at school. One more year under the confining and sheltering gaze of teachers and school rules; one more year and the world would, quite literally, be at their feet.

'We do this as a team remember?' Emotion betrayed the calmness of Liz's voice.

'Course, always.'

A leaf littered path stretched in front of them, the fallen foliage blanketing the trail in a natural waft and wave pattern. Like an open book, it beckoned them forward, guiding them toward a mysterious door that was nestled into a solid rock face. This unusual gateway lacked a handle and seemed out of proportion to the space surrounding it. Firmly settled at its centre was a keyhole and it was this unassuming chasm that demanded attention.

Ready for the challenge, John's free hand reached down to cover Liz's, and thus united, they placed the key into the lock and turned. The ancient door creaked open, radiating a silent welcome.

'Sweet,' John exclaimed with customary eagerness.

Equally enthusiastic, albeit somewhat more watchful, Liz gazed down towards their destination. Far below a small stage rose from the base of the funnel-like scaffold. The climb down would not be easy, but they were ready. This was their adventure, all they needed to do was place their feet on the waiting ladder.

Side by side Liz and John reached for the first foothold. They eased their way down, slowly and deliberately grasping the metal bars of the scaffold, grateful for the solid support offered. As their legs guided them down power seemed to rise from their feet, up their legs to the knees that flexed in coordination, sending raw energy into their quads. They continued to climb down, each step taking them closer to the platform below.

'What if there's nothing down there.' It was only momentary, but the fleeting loss of concentration had cost momentum, Liz lost her footing and slipped. She screamed in desperation as her arms flailed wildly in a frantic search for something solid.

There was only air.

'Liz!'

John felt the icy fingers of fear tighten around his chest. Frantically he tried to grab her hand.

And missed.

The panic escalated.

'Liz! Reach! REACH!'

Thwack!

The structure shuddered as Liz's right hand made contact and curled around a solid bar. Her left hand followed and she hung suspended for a moment before finally finding her footing on a lower rung.

Like a monkey, John scampered down to reach her. He moved across to cocoon her small frame within his own. He held her gently as shivers of terror wracked her body.

'I'm here.' He repeated softly, 'I'm here.'

'I'm scared,' Liz whispered. 'We don't know what's down there. We don't know who's down there. I can't do this. I can't move, I don't think I have the strength.'

'Liz, we have to take this one step at a time. We can go back up to where we started, or we can go on. Either way we have to make a choice. We can't just stand still and wait. There is a world of opportunity waiting for us; maybe it's just a little way further down. I know there is courage in you. Focus on that. Just breathe.'

Breathe.
Fully aware.
Breathe.

Liz allowed John's words to soothe, mending the chasm of fear with a bridge of hope. The unknown dread was replaced with faith and she nodded.

'Okay.'

Slowly they continued the downward climb. Each carefully placed step drawing them closer to their destination.

'Almost there.'

John's feet touched the solid platform and he held out his arms to steady Liz as she took her final step to join him.

'We're there.'

As if on cue, lights appeared in the scaffolding above and behind them. Bright spirals of colour swooped and swirled, encasing the pair in a shower of light. Then, as if someone had turned a kaleidoscope, the colours dimmed and before them stretched a vast luminous space.

Welcome to the World of Expression.

Chapter 1

The KEY

An Introduction to the Concepts:

Setting *MyStory*

What is *MyStory*?

Primarily, *MyStory* is a map that encourages you to actively and consciously direct your own life. The stories, information and strategies contained within its pages demonstrate how being aware of our actions and recognising that we are responsible and accountable for our own behaviour, places us in a position of control rather than *being* controlled.

MyStory will encourage you to stop believing that someone else dictates what you think, feel and do and, instead, show you how you can become the master of your own thoughts, feelings and actions. Thus, in a metaphorical sense, *MyStory* offers a scaffold for you to write your own story rather than being a character in someone else's. While it is true that you may not be able to control your environment, as the author you can choose the direction of your thoughts, you can manage your emotions and you can select your actions. Alternatively, you may like to think of becoming the programmer of your own hard drive, or the explorer on your own trail.

To help you on your creative path, *MyStory* offers theories, questions and, most importantly, stories. As you have probably recognised, you will also encounter metaphors. These metaphors form the basis of a purposeful strategy that aims to illuminate less visible concepts. In fact, each of the stories in *MyStory* is in itself a metaphor. Their inclusion is designed to show you how metaphors can be used to provide a deeper understanding of the thought processes and emotions that underpin your actions.

Therefore at a secondary level, *MyStory* also opens the door to a lifelong learning strategy. It uses narrative, propelled by metaphors and mindfulness, to promote critical literacy. As you read, answer questions, adopt the techniques and practise the strategies, you can increase your capacity to become a confident, courageous, compassionate and creative individual.

Nevertheless, even though *MyStory* offers you a key, it will be your choice to place that key in the lock, turn it, open the door and step through into a wider world of expression. This is your inner domain. It is the place of self and access to it requires action. It is up to you to put in the effort.

Why Read *MyStory*?

The creation of this scaffold is built on the premise that 'prevention is better than cure'. In other words, as a young person reading this you will uncover the powerful resources within. This is your generator. You may like to think of it as the place within yourself where you can find confidence, courage, compassion and creativity. These attributes can provide the power to energise your life. The inspirational energy they provide can illuminate your learning path; your path to wellbeing and success.

If you are an adult or parent reading this, you can recover the young person within yourself and, as you begin to accept that young person, you can gain a greater understanding of the young people in your life. Acceptance and understanding are prerequisites for growth. What will grow and flourish here are your relationships.

But how is this book different from the countless other self-help and personal development books available?

It isn't. *But it is!*

Personal development literature is largely based on a central principle: that of looking within yourself and becoming confident and strong while drawing support from a higher purpose. As you identify, accept and love who you are, you become responsible for yourself and thus become the author of your own life rather than a character in someone else's.

However, social attitudes towards personal development and living a successful, fulfilled life often seem to be contradictory, with some advocating self-esteem, love of self, and a belief that anything that can be thought of can be achieved; while others promote the need to experience failure and learn that not everyone is special. The role of happiness in our lives is debated while many are absorbed with achievement and a number on a page. Over all looms the spectre of technology and a compulsion to compete.

Therefore, rather than adopting a psychologist persona, a coach's personality or an entrepreneurial mantle, the approach offered in this book is grounded in my experience as a secondary school English teacher. It provides a scaffold which combines familiar learning strategies with fresh perspectives. I have used stories to illustrate and substantiate less familiar territories. My years of teaching have shown me time and time again that profound learning about self and relationships is possible though connection to stories. We are surrounded by stories. They have facilitated the transmission of traditions and the recounting of history. Narrative entertains us and has been popular throughout human history.

Have you ever heard the expression, 'You are today what you'll be five years from now, except for the people you meet and the books you read'?

If this is true (and I tend to believe it is) our reading and viewing affects the people we become. Think about it this way – what we read and watch today will influence who we become tomorrow. To put this into some kind of perspective I would like to offer a personal experience. During my childhood and teen years I probably watched the movie *Mary Poppins* at least five or six times. Then later I watched it with my children, but this time I watched it through parent/teacher eyes. The impact was mind blowing. Here, in a neat, simple narrative, was the message to live life purposefully, thoughtfully, cheerfully and ethically while still appreciating the magic of actually living. As a child I simply enjoyed the positive feeling it inspired. As an adult I realised this was a valuable message for any young mind.

I like to think that movies such as *Mary Poppins, Chitty Chitty Bang Bang* and *The Sound of Music*, coupled with books such as the 'Trixie Belden' and 'Silver Brumby' series, as well as *Heidi, Anne of Green Gables* and *The Naughtiest Girl at School,* influenced the person I have become. They instilled a sense of moral responsibility, an individual accountability and a recognition of the cooperation and consideration required within relationships. They stimulated a sense of wonder and a willingness to believe in what I could not see. They inspired my love and respect of nature. They encouraged my sense of positivity. They supported my family values.

Equally significant was a gift from my father – a small poster with a poem printed on it – that had a profound impact on my life. The poem, by an anonymous poet, was called 'A Smile'. As I was growing up, this poster hung on the inside of my wardrobe door and I looked at it every morning. The poem began with the lines:

A smile costs nothing but gives much.
It enriches those who receive
Without making poorer those who give

It ended with the lines:

Some people are too tired to give you a smile,
Give them one of yours ...

For as long as I can remember, people have commented on my smile. In fact, during my entire secondary school experience I was known not as Nicole, but as 'Smiley'. I realise now that looking at that poem every morning and every evening, I was unconsciously embedding within myself a value, a way of living my life. It has always been important for me to share a smile with those I meet.

15

I like to think this simple act of smiling enabled me to nurture the optimistic attitude that has guided me throughout my life.

How consciously do you read?

What can you learn
from stories?

How to Read *MyStory*

In order to gain maximum benefits from your reading, first ask yourself what you expect to achieve. Then become comfortable with the ideas and strategies as you enjoy reading the stories. Finally, consolidate your new skills through questioning and practice.

Mentally Prepare

The key to learning a new skill is first to generate the desire to have that skill and the intention to perfect it, then you must commit to purposeful action. So ask yourself:

- Why have I chosen to read this book?
- What do I hope to gain?
- How willing am I to implement what I learn?

Read Attentively

- Note your emotional responses to what you are reading, particularly when reading the stories (write these responses in the margins; use words such as 'funny', 'irritating', or 'unsure').
- Relate the information you read to incidents from your own experience.
- Reflect on your past reactions and how you behaved in similar circumstances.
- Question if you would behave differently now.

Actively Learn

- Write comments or notes in the margins (e.g. 'check this' or 'try this later').
- Underline sentences that have particular meaning for you.

- Complete the questions and exercises listed in the <u>Reflect</u> and <u>Approach</u> sections.
- View the movies (or the movie extracts) suggested.

Instructions for Reflect Section

The <u>Reflect</u> sections of *MyStory* remind you to explore what you are thinking and how you are feeling. They show you that it is possible to watch or read your thoughts and feelings from an objective perspective. The latter parts of *MyStory* encourage you to use these skills to develop a sense of mindfulness. It is a good idea to physically write your answers to these questions.

Instruction for Approach Sections

The <u>Approach</u> sections require in-depth action. The questions ask you to act purposefully and complete the exercises. You will find the more committed you are to completing these activities, the more benefits you will receive from reading this book.

Remember

We have all heard from people who blather on about the books they have read and courses they have attended. However, if the knowledge gained from these books or courses is not actively applied it is all but useless. The simple fact remains, the fire of desire to become better can ignite success but without resolute action, the fire soon dies. Thus, knowledge must be actively applied in order to be useful. Learning is an active process.

In an age of instant change, mastering the art of learning is essential. This is why learning how to learn is so powerful.

Embark on a quest to reveal your *MyStory*.

Use this scaffold as a map
to find the key which unlocks the door
to the powerful resources within.

The assembly of these resources
will provide you with the tools
for lifelong learning
so you can GRASP your future.

GRASP the Story

Before we continue, I would like to introduce you to a learning strategy that can help you develop your critical literacy skills. This is one step towards taking control of your own learning. It is an approach I have used in the classroom for many years and it involves making a commitment to GRASP your life.

GRASP

G = Gather data from a variety of sources – read, watch, listen and discuss. Be alert to what is happening around you so you can collect information and ideas from diverse angles.

R = Reflect on the data you have assembled. Think about the information and view it from numerous perspectives. Challenge or accept ideas as you compare them to your own values, experiences and learnings in different areas.

A = Analyse the data you have collected. Break the information down into its component parts and test its reliability, credibility and accuracy. Ask questions about the author's audience, context and purpose.

S = Synthesise data and your values. Choose and rearrange the information, thoughts and ideas in new and imaginative ways that merge harmoniously with your values.

P = Propose your own ideas based on your synthesis. Be bold, creative and courageous enough to form your own reasoned opinions based on diverse, tangible evidence.

Observing student behaviour over the past 14 years has shown me that the students who GRASP information have chosen to:

- be actively aware in class.
- be self-motivated.
- be curious when discovering links between topics and subjects.
- be reflective when presented with new ideas.
- persevere when learning new information and skills.
- have courage when sharing their ideas, thoughts and feelings.

It seems to me that many of the most successful students have also decided to:

- be consciously aware of their surroundings and be present in the moment.
- conduct themselves with honesty and integrity.
- accept themselves for who they are.
- be the best version of themselves.

What will you choose?

Story – Making a Commitment

Mary was a Year 11 student who read feverishly, eagerly immersing herself in the pages. She willingly participated in class discussions, sharing her ideas and commenting on the relationship between themes and real life. Her observations reflected an in-depth understanding of what she had read and an ability to critically evaluate a situation. However, her writing lacked conviction. Ideas were presented in a random way with little thought to sentence structure or presenting a cohesive argument. Mary relied on colloquial expression and often just retold the story, rather than offering critical analysis. During lessons where Mary was required to write, she chatted with her classmates, either dissecting last weekend's activities, or planning the weekend ahead. When asked by her teacher, Mr Miln, to focus on her work, Mary became sullen and uncooperative.

Mr Miln was an experienced teacher who had encountered many students like Mary during his 15 years of teaching. He wanted to help Mary improve her writing skills so she could achieve the results she was capable of. Yet every time he talked about essay-writing skills, Mary was more interested in her classmates or gazing out the window. So Mr Miln raised his concerns at a parent-teacher evening. Mary angrily accused him of playing favourites in class and singling her out for undue criticism. Mary's parents wanted to support their daughter, yet they were aware her examination results had always been poor. Sitting across from two sets of anxious eyes and one set of furious ones, Mr Miln made a decision. He realised he was tired of rehashing the same conciliatory discussion year after year with students who felt threatened and parents who felt confused. This is the moment, he thought. This is the moment where either I stop teaching altogether or I start *really* teaching.

Smiling gently he leant across the table towards Mary and her parents. Speaking softly he asked her, 'What are you afraid of?'

Mary returned his earnest gaze with a look of incredulous indignation. How dare he accuse her of being scared!

Again Mr Miln repeated his question. 'Mary, what are you afraid of?'

With a toss of her head Mary snapped, 'Nothing.'

Satisfied, Mr Miln settled back in his chair and nodded. 'I thought so.'

Mary's eyes widened as Mr Miln continued, 'Mary you have so much to offer. Your ideas are valuable and should be shared. But this fear of nothing, this belief that you have nothing valuable to offer, is crippling you.

'That's not what I said,' Mary replied angrily. 'You are twisting my words.'

Again Mr Miln smiled gently. 'Am I? You told us you were scared of nothing, and from what I see that is exactly what we need to explore. It seems to me that when you are faced with a blank sheet of paper you see an expanse of nothing and that is frightening.'

He checked to see he had her attention before continuing. 'As you gaze at that blank page you are scared. You begin to think that it reflects a nothingness in you. So you search for ways to find connections and affirmations from the people sitting around you. Alternatively, you gaze out the window imagining all the things you would like to write about but don't want to since putting them on paper means others will have tangible evidence of your thoughts.'

Mr Miln paused briefly before adding, 'Mary, it seems to me that you fear your ideas are just more "nothing" so you convince yourself it is better to write nothing than be accused of writing ideas that are worth nothing.'

Chapter 1: The Key

Mary squirmed uncomfortably in her seat but remained silent, so Mr Miln kept speaking. 'Mary, what would happen if you redirected those fears? What would happen if you believed in yourself and had confidence in your ideas – after all, they are your ideas and all anyone else can say is that they do not share your opinion. Ultimately, a difference of opinion is simply that, a *different* opinion.'

Mary was leaning forward in her seat now, so Mr Miln offered a little more. 'I want you to feel free to express yourself. I want to provide you with a supportive place where you can develop your skills. A safe environment where your dreams can become tangible realities. But I need your help. I need you to make a conscious decision that you want to share your ideas in writing by presenting coherent, sophisticated arguments that can be judged by others. Judgement is something to be embraced. It is through listening to others that we begin to sense the multiple perspectives that make up our world and it is by appreciating those multiple perspectives that we grow.'

Mary blinked a few times before offering a half smile. 'Mr Miln,' she said shyly, 'I want to write better, but every time I try, I get back results saying I have not answered the question, or my language is too simple, or my sentences don't make sense.'

Mr Miln nodded. 'So ... how do you feel when you hear those comments?'

Mary answered slowly, 'I feel worthless and that all my effort was for nothing.'

Again Mr Miln nodded. 'So what do you do with those feelings?'

Mary thought a moment before responding. Pointing to her stomach she said, 'I shove them down here and think I don't care.'

Mr Miln looked Mary in the eye and asked, 'Why?'

Mary shook her head and responded plaintively, 'Because it hurts to care.'

Mr Miln looked back at Mary's parents, who had been earnestly listening to this exchange, before returning his attention to Mary. 'Mary, this is what we need to address. I can show you how to write sentences that make sense. I can provide strategies for answering a question. I can even teach you how to use sophisticated language. But you need to care. You need to care about yourself. You need to believe in yourself rather than looking for external reassurances.'

Again he looked at Mary's parents. 'Look, I realise this is a lot to ask of a young lady who is still discovering who she is. I realise developing a sense of inner trust is a lifelong process, but the earlier we start, the more equipped we are to live *our* life.'

Mary's parents nodded. Mr Miln smiled. 'So Mary what do you say? Are you willing to care and have faith in yourself? Remember, I will be here to offer support.'

He stopped and thought for a moment. 'Do you remember learning to ride a bike? You may have been anxious. You may even have fallen off a few times and been frightened to get back on.'

Mary's father chuckled. 'That's right. Remember you said you were never going to ride a bike again so I may as well sell it. I asked you to give it another go and reassured you that I would hold on to the back of the bike and run along beside you. You were reluctant, but you also wanted the freedom that riding a bike offered. So, you pedalled and I held on running next to you. In no time at all you were riding on your own.'

Mary looked at her father. 'Yes, Dad, I do remember.'

Three sets of expectant eyes now looked at Mr Miln as he said, 'Well, Mary, just like a bike gives you the freedom to go to places on your own, confident writing gives you the freedom to express your ideas and to refine and clarify your thinking. Do you want that?'

Mary nodded, so he continued. 'Okay, I'll support you by giving you a structure – a scaffold to hang your ideas on – no more beginning with "nothing". But you will have to respond with definite purpose, willingness to practise and confidence in your ability to achieve.'

Mary's half smile widened to a grin as she nodded. 'Yes, Mr Miln, I will.'

Are you ready to approach the door?

Will you use the key?

Preparation for *MyStory*

Like Mary, you need to make a commitment to yourself:

- Are you willing to have confidence in your ability to achieve?
- Are you willing to respond with definite purpose?
- Are you willing to practise?

Remember, to fully experience the magic of *MyStory* immerse yourself in the reading experience. Even though there may be occasions when you wonder where the words are taking you, keep reading. Sometimes it takes time for a clear picture to form. Think for a moment – have you ever watched a movie that seemed to twist and turn and then invert in on itself before revealing the final message? (Movies such as *The Matrix* or *Inception* spring to mind.) Generally stories such as these intrigue us because we need to watch for details. They maintain our interest because we are called to solve a puzzle.

So be aware that as you read the next few pages you are moving towards a space where you can begin to create your own *MyStory*. In this sense, Chapter 1 of this scaffold establishes setting and mood. It is the introductory or orientation chapter which aims to open your mind to fresh perspectives and to broaden your mindset. The more flexibility and imagination you contribute, the more actively and thoughtfully involved you will be in your learning process.

Whose story is it?

A demonstration of how easy it is
to fall into the Character Trap.

The Character Trap

It is easy to fall into the trap of following the stories laid down for us. First we mimic our parents (our values and perceptions are most powerfully established from birth till the age of 7), then we copy or imitate what we see around us (ages 7 – 14), finally we are influenced by our peers (ages 14 – 21). So, by the time we emerge to seize a measure of influence over our own life, we have already been programmed by family, peers and society.

Although is true that parents, teachers, mentors and friends have much to offer in terms of support and guidance, it is important to recognise whose life we are living, because all too often, the quest to fulfil someone else's expectation leads to a place of frustration, resentment and perhaps even a perception of failure. My own story offers an example.

As a child, I wanted to be a teacher. I would incessantly plague a tolerant cousin, three years my senior, to play Schools for hours on end.

However, at 15, I allowed my story to be rewritten by a boyfriend destined to be a merchant banker. I allowed him to substitute my dreams for his.

I allowed.

Why?

First, I permitted him to instil uncertainty. 'Why would you want to become a teacher? No-one respects teachers and the pay is pitiful.'

Then I accepted his alternative path. 'You could study marketing and become someone with influence.'

I let him alter my course.

Why?

He gave me a story, and I chose to live it, rather than writing my own. I trusted his version of my life. It became tangible because he gave it to me. I could read it and follow it, rather than creating something from the intangible forces within myself. His option seemed safer. It implied acceptance. If he read my life that way, so should I. After all I trusted him, I loved him.

Didn't I?

Following his story meant I didn't have to use my imagination or creativity. I simply had to do as I was told.

But a line from Robert Frost's poem 'The Road Not Taken' resonated within me.

Two roads diverged in a wood, and I –
I took the one less travelled by ...

I felt compelled to choose the less travelled path, to be different, to rebel against conformity. Yet I felt obligated to meet the expectations of my childhood sweetheart, friends, teachers and, of course, my parents. As a result I was frustrated, confused and directionless.

Perhaps this was why my brother accused me of being a seeker. He argued that if I constantly sought I would never find. His point was valid. I needed to decide on a destination. More importantly, I needed to be able to recognise when I got there.

Who was I? Where did I want to be?

I wanted to teach, I wanted to write. I dreamed of living in a sun-drenched home, a place where I could write, gaze out over the water and contribute towards making the world a just place.

Chapter 1: The Key

So I decided to take responsibility for my own actions. I chose to be the writer of my own story rather than the character in someone else's. And now I live on an island in the middle of a city. I enjoy days sitting on my balcony reading and writing. I look out over the river, to my left is the ocean, to my right, are rolling bush covered hills. I am in *my* Paradise.

Would you like

to be the author of your own life

rather than a character in someone else's?

MyStory: A Rite

Imagine being born into a clearing,
choosing a trail and
embarking on a quest.

Which trail will you choose?
Does a compass direct your choice?

Imagine the destination
Is the river of life,
And the endless ocean.

Notice how the track
winds its way
through the forest,
branching off in many directions.

Can you see
the intersecting paths;
crossroads of choice?

Can you see, hear
and feel
what is happening around you?

Be aware of the sounds
that coax you off course.
Where is the compass which offers
direction?

During childhood, teen and early adult life we stride, meander, creep, slide and tiptoe through the forest. Then, as we approach middle years we reach a river; our outlook expands and we begin to notice and experience the intangible ebbs and flows around us.

Some chose to remain in the forest, clinging to childhood, or wild adolescence. Others fall into a stream and fight desperately against the currents. They wield their paddles like a weapon in a desperate attempt to force their direction.

Some wade into the river and welcome the opportunity to flow with the tide; they draw strength from the compass within and navigate toward their destination, choosing the natural tributaries to merge into a greater river.

Maybe, as we approach our older years, we can recline, secure and trusting that, as our quest ends, we may flow peacefully within the river and move toward an eternal sea.

Is our quest predestined? This question is worthy of contemplation and has frequently been explored through literature. In *Romeo and Juliet* Shakespeare ponders the question through the voice of the chorus who introduces Romeo and Juliet as 'A pair of star-crossed lovers'[1]; lovers who were destined to suffer. Yet later in the play, this time through the voice of Friar Lawrence, we are told, 'Within the infant rind of this weak flower / Poison hath residence, and medicine power.'[2] In other words, a situation has the potential to be helpful or unhelpful, depending on the choices made.

What is the connection between destiny and the opportunity for simultaneous helpfulness and unhelpfulness? Were Romeo and Juliet destined to die and reunite their warring families? Did their innocent love have the potential to either inspire or destroy, depending on the choices they made?

---

[1] William Shakespeare, *Romeo and Juliet*, Act 1, Prologue, ln 9.

[2] William Shakespeare, *Romeo and Juliet*, Act 2, Sc3, ln 19-20.

Your answers to these questions offer insights into your internal belief systems. As you uncover these belief systems, your internal compass may be revealed.

Take a moment now to consider your beliefs about destiny, choice (free will) and the relationship between perspective, optimism and pessimism.

Reflect

1. Do you believe destiny is 'written in the stars' or do our choices choose our destiny?

2. Which choices are within your sphere of control? What choices can you make, as you travel the Learning Path?

Navigate the *Learning Path,*
be the author
of your own
MyStory.

The Learning Path

Henry Ford once said:

> *Anyone who stops learning is old, whether at twenty or eighty. Anyone who keeps learning stays young. The greatest thing in life is to keep your mind young.*

In other words learning occurs throughout life and, if we stop learning, or relinquish the will to learn, we no longer 'live'.

In keeping with this concept, I would like to suggest that we also need to experience life, in order to 'really live'. This idea was one of the central themes in the movie *Dead Poets Society*. The teacher, Mr Keating, encourages his students to reflect upon the words of Henry David Thoreau:

> *I went to the woods because I wished to live deliberately, to front only the essential facts of life, and see if I could not learn what it had to teach, and not, when I came to die, discover that I had not lived.*

As an English teacher, I love using stories such as *Dead Poets Society* to explore the 'act of living'. Through stories it is possible to enter a new world and participate from a protected position so that, when a character learns, we learn. Often, the world of creative expression may seem like a place where the rules constantly shift; a place where promises are made then broken and prizes attained only to disintegrate in the face of a perceived truth. However, as we wander through the layers of the story and discover delight in the experience, encountering the world of narrative becomes fuel for the imagination. It unlocks inner inspiration and offers alternative perspectives.

Of course, it would not be wise to live only within the pages of a book. (Films such as *The Lion, the Witch and the Wardrobe, Jumanji* and *Bedtime Stories,* explore this idea nicely.) Certainly it is important to live and be aware in the present. However, as we analyse the characters in a story and critically evaluate the strategies they employ to overcome complications, we may gain a fresh perspective of our own situation. If we are open we may also begin to perceive some innovative solutions. Therefore, critically reading stories encourages readers to propose questions and discover answers.

This is the 'Art of Learning'.

As you know, the law of gravity states that what rises must fall. Similarly, life may be described as a series of ups and downs, challenges and rewards or disappointments and pleasures. One of my favourite analogies is that of the heart rate monitor which blips the peaks and troughs of the heart's systolic and diastolic rhythm (and remember, a flatline indicates life has left). Perhaps a more peaceful image is the Yin Yang symbol which represents the opposing yet complementary forces which simultaneously offer momentum and balance. Or the cross offered by Christianity to convey the concepts of love and sacrifice. In other words, life is not a flat, smooth road. Rather, it is a series of rolling hills, rugged mountains, sprawling plains, calm oases and swirling rivers. The path through these spaces may be described as

the Learning Path.

I believe the process of learning reaches into the core of human activity. Learning promotes balance and supports life. The ability to learn and, perhaps more importantly, feeling confident in our ability to learn, provides us with the courage and compassion to enjoy life without being bound by fear. We dare to dream because learning allows us to reframe our perceptions. When we encounter a barrier or challenge, we take the learning and keep pushing forward. This builds resilience and confidence.

Learning places a *Master Key* in our hand.

You have probably heard the saying 'learning is a lifelong process'. Certainly in today's world of rapidly developing technology, the ability to learn new ideas, skills, systems and processes seems to be essential for survival.

However, when were you actually taught how to learn? At school you may study subjects such as English, Maths, Science, History, Geography, Commerce, Computing, Art, Music and Physical Education. But how many of these classes actually taught you the processes involved in learning? Often when we are at school, we are so busy remembering content and developing skills that we do not pause to reflect upon the processes that ensure we remember that content or develop those skills. Yet ... the most important skill we can learn at school is

how to learn.

Luckily, learning is a skill, therefore it can be taught and it can be learnt. It is a process that can be practised. When we know the steps involved in our own learning processes, we build self-reliance. When we know how to learn we gain the capacity to respond to the changes that will inevitably occur within our environment; and this makes us feel confident. With this confidence comes the

courage to be creative

and the

peace to be compassionate.

41

When we know how to learn, we become the author of our own life, rather than the character in someone else's because we have the confidence and creativity to see our future and the courage and compassion to live it.

There are many different theories about learning and it is not my intention to explore them in detail here. Rather, I would like to introduce you to the *Learning Path* and suggest some strategies which will help you navigate it. With each step you will be learning about how you learn.

Would you like to step onto
the *Learning Path?*

This is a
conscious action
that involves
recognising
self-responsibility.

It will take
**focus, persistence,
flexibility, commitment,**
and
determination.

The *Learning Path* to *MyStory*

Step 1   Find yourself
In the author's space

Step 2   4C your future
Confidence, courage, creativity, compassion

Step 3   Discover your own place
Settle comfortably within yourself

Step 4   Navigate with your *Honour Compass*
Sync and balance

Step 5   Allow your emotions
Be emotionally aware

Step 6   Manage your emotions
Monitor how you really feel

Step 7   Acknowledge your thoughts
Be thoughtfully present

Step 8   Define your direction
Set your target

Step 9   Take a breath
Breathe mindfully

Step 10   Cultivate an aware mind
Critically reading and writing

An Exercise in Imagination ...

Imagine opening a door and standing on the threshold
with no idea where you are,
what you want or
where you are going.

How do you feel?

You may feel uncertain about the threats which lie ahead.
You may feel anxious about the prospect of meeting new people.
You may doubt your ability to respond to the challenges in front
of you.

or

You may feel optimistic about the opportunities which lie ahead.
You may feel excited about the prospect of meeting new people.
You may feel confident in your ability to respond to the
adventure in front of you.

Regardless, you are likely to wonder,

'What am I going to do?'

Is This *MyStory*

Imagine how you will feel when someone hands you a map.
A map is a tool that provides direction. It offers tangible guidance.

Now imagine being placed in the middle of a forest
                                        with that map,

                        but without any clues as to
                        where you are.

                                How will you proceed?

Your map needs a 'you are here' signpost.

                        Then you can choose where you want to go.

However, to ensure you reach your destination

                        you will also need a guidance system.

Chapter 1: The Key

As you immerse yourself within the pages of *MyStory* you are being presented with a key to open your door. You are being handed a map to chart your way. This map offers an opportunity to uncover your *Honour Compass* so that you may consciously travel your *Learning Path*.

As you read, you will also be encouraged to collect the 4C-ing tools of confidence, courage, creativity and compassion. These attributes can help you proceed along your *Learning Path* so that you may become the author of your *MyStory*.

Are you ready to walk through the door,

locate your generator and

uncover your compass?

Chapter 2

The DOOR

Accessing the Inner Realm

Choose to Write *MyStory*

Choose to Write Your Own *MyStory*

The ideas, stories and exercises in this chapter of the scaffold are offered to assist you explore the territories within you. They propose theories, suggest perspectives and ask questions so you can navigate your internal pathways. You may like to think of these pathways as the codes which comprise your internal programs or the themes of your internal world of expression. Familiarity with these internal pathways improves your ability to plot your path through the external world.

Who am I?	A sense of self.
	This involves identifying the character traits, belief systems and values that influence the choices you make.
Where am I *Where do I* *want to be?*	A sense of place and destination. This entails determining a place and purpose that will provide you with security and direction.
How will I *get there?*	A moral compass This requires choosing a path and charting a planned approach that syncs and balances who you are, with your personal values and where you want to be.

Your responsibility is to actively involve yourself in the process; make a commitment to answer the questions and complete the exercises.

Are you ready to travel the Learning Path
and access the Inner Realm?

Story: The Rite I

It was a test. She knew it was a test, one she wanted to complete, a contest that had been eagerly anticipated. But now that it was time, she just felt cold.

She knew her ancestors had faced this same moment. And survived.

Would she?

Tania searched memories for comfort and reassurance, but all that returned was … loneliness.

Which way?

She belonged to an ancient tribe, from an ancient place; their customs and traditions unfamiliar to a modern world. However, here, in the riotous wilderness of the forest, tests which measured an individual's ability to face the future seemed appropriate.

The test she faced today was the one reserved for the strongest members of the tribe – the Warrior's Rite. Although it was an honour to be chosen, it was also a source of nightmare. Each year fewer returned. No-one knew why.

But Tania wanted to know. *Had* to know.
Why?

Why did so many leave, and so few return?

Slinging the bow strap across her shoulder, she recalled her preparation. In her mind she repacked her bag, ticking off an imaginary checklist to reassure herself she had sufficient supplies.
Water – check
Dried meat – check
Arrows – check

Knife – check
Extra set of skins – check
Ropes - check
Clue where she was going – No

That's not entirely true, Tania reminded herself. I know which direction to take, I know where the path starts, I know why I am doing this, I just don't know what to expect.

'Does it matter?' The question appeared from nowhere and hung like a wraith awaiting a response.

Maybe not. Tania's reply fell into the empty space ahead and grinning at her own audacity, she began. Placing one moccasined foot in front of the other she walked out of the village towards the glowing horizon. It would soon be night.

Cold ...

Dark ...

Oh no! Flint! Did I remember the flint?

Anxious moments of doubt threatened to overpower as she agonised over options without a fire. No spark, no warmth, nothing to keep the darkness at bay.

'Except yourself,' the spectral voice returned.

Except myself.

Relief.

And yes, I did pack a flint.

Shaking off visions of tragic scenarios, Tania focused her attention on what lay ahead. *I am ready for this. I have trained for this. I asked for this.* Her thoughts became a mantra and Tania felt a reassuring rush of self-assurance.

Chapter 2: The Door

I am ready for this.
I have trained for this.
I asked for this.

As the darkness closed around her, the moon became her ally.
With growing confidence, Tania walked into the waiting shadows.

<u>Step 1 on the *Learning Path*</u>

Find yourself
in the author's space

Are you ready to look inside
to the author within?

Step 1: Find Yourself in the Author's Space

In order to write your own *MyStory* you need to accept yourself
as the author. This requires you to reflect upon your own internal
representations. In other words, how do you perceive yourself,
what do you see as your strengths and weaknesses. Ask yourself,
how these attitudes were formed? Could it be that they echo the
impressions of others, rather than being what you know to be true
about your authentic self? Also consider how you feel.

Do you sometimes feel conflicted, anxious or out of balance?

The outcome you are striving for is a deeper understanding of self.
This should lead you to the discovery of your internal resource
generator. This generator is your personal power source and offers
the potential for wider connections. At its core is confidence,
courage, compassion and creativity. Your generator is fuelled
by GRASP (refer to page 21) and must be actively maintained
through downloads and shareware (this will become clearer as you
read on). For now, simply imagine that your generator is a power
source from which you draw the energy to achieve whatever it is
you choose to achieve. Notice how I said 'choose to achieve'?
Remember, you are the author, the programmer, the traveller, so
you direct the action.

As the teacher, it is my role to divide the process of discovering
who you are into manageable and recognisable sections that may
be easily digested. So, as you read these pages, I am handing you
key codes, but as you know, you will need to input the data. This
is an active chapter of the book. It requires a choice to become
the author. So, place yourself in the author's space and answer the
questions that follow.

Reflect

Think carefully about each of the questions below. Remember in this section it is important to actually write (or type) your responses. The physical act of writing helps you to consolidate your thoughts. In other words, your thoughts become a physical entity that you can see and touch. Therefore they become tangible and manageable.

1. How would you describe yourself?

2. How would you describe your story thus far?

3. What do you enjoy doing?

4. What specifically do you enjoy about this activity?

5. Who do you admire?

6. Which qualities do you admire in that person?

7. Which of your internal qualities (personality traits) do you value?

8. When do you feel confident sharing your skills with others?

9. What is your ultimate dream? (Move beyond 'reality', be creative and stretch your imagination.)

10. Suggest some skills that you can develop to achieve this dream.

11. How would you explain the meaning of the phrases:
    • Seek and you will find.
    • Reap what you sow.

<u>Who am I?</u>

I am a teacher.
A teacher is who I am.
I love being a teacher.
I love to teach.

I am a writer.
A writer is who I am.
I love being a writer.
I love to write.

I am a mother.
I am a lover.
I am a daughter.
I am a sister.
I am a friend.
I am a colleague.
I am a citizen.

I am a writer who teaches.
A dreamer who smiles.
A believer who cares.

Chapter 2: The Door

The simple act of writing this poem was intensely liberating; it was my catalyst for increased self-awareness. Although it took some time to compose, the action of reflection and physically writing my thoughts freed me from the shackles of expectations. This was the day I recognised myself as a writer and celebrated the fact that I was a teacher. It was the day I started living the life of my choice. I realised this was my authentic self. I opened a door to feel the sun shine brightly on my face and a gentle breeze embrace my body; it felt as though the world smiled and gave me a hug.

Writing soothes my soul and frees my spirit. I have learnt that I must write in order to feel alive. The compulsion to create through the written word is like a tangible force that demands recognition. Without writing I feel isolated and directionless. Writing offers me purpose.

However – and this is important – I write for myself. I journal and I write to make sense of my thoughts. The inspiration and the accolades come from within. As a result, it doesn't matter how others perceive my writing. Although it is gratifying when they enjoy what I wrote or compliment my expression, I do not write for praise. I write because a writer is who I am.

Why have I shared this with you? To encourage you to search inside yourself to discover what it is you love to do. As you explore your passion you are likely to learn more about your own motivations and de-motivations. This may be your first step toward discovering your inner inspiration.

Reflect

1. What are you passionate about?

2. What makes you feel

   i) happy?

   ii) inspired?

   iii) energised?

   iv) complete?

Chapter 2: The Door

Approach

Remember you can quite literally 'reap what you sow'. In other words, the more willing you are to purposefully complete the exercises, the more benefits you will receive. Imagine achieving success on the sporting field, dance studio or even the virtual gaming world. You know that it would be very difficult to become a world class footballer, a prima ballerina, or a master gamer simply by watching others or reading a 'how to' manual. You know that success and improved performance occurs as a result of 'doing'. So do!

Write: Begin a *MyStory* journal. This may be 'hard copy', such as a hard cover spiral-bound note book, or it may be personal blog site. For tips on how to set up a blog visit www.isthismystory.com

Write a short reflection in your journal or blog now. In your reflection explore your impression of yourself.

Then, at the end of each MyStory chapter, invest the time to write another short reflection.

Create: Construct an ideal vision of you. In other words, the version of you that you want to be. You may like to:

- write a poem
- write a short story
- paint or draw a picture
- create a collage of images cut from magazines or from the internet
- design a glog (graphical blog).

Step 2 on the *Learning Path*

4C your future
confidence, courage, creativity, compassion

Step 1 *encouraged you to peer inside yourself and discover who you are.*

Now it is time for the second step.

Are you ready to
4C your future?

Step 2: 4C Your Future

If you say '4C' out aloud it sounds very similar to the word 'foresee', and to foresee means to see in advance or, in some contexts, to predict.

Would you like to foresee your future?

To be very clear, I am *not* talking about paranormal activity. Rather I am encouraging you to dream about or visualise the future you would like to live. Visualisation is a popular success-building technique within most sports. For example, many footballers, athletes, cricketers, netballers, basketballers, gymnasts, golfers and swimmers use visualisation to focus their attention and train their bodies. Their aim is to experience what it would be like to score the winning point, land the perfect manoeuvre or win the ultimate race. Similarly, many personal development courses recommend visualisation to strengthen goal-setting activities. Even the opening pages of this book asked you to participate in a visualisation exercise.

Why?

One purpose of a visualisation is to create neural pathways or connections within the brain. These link a current state of being to a desired state of being. Keeping the explanation simple this means that by visualising what you would like to occur, you are also completing a mental warm-up. In other words, you are preparing your brain to process the thoughts and emotions required to instruct your body to perform the actions necessary to achieve whatever it is you would like to achieve.

A second purpose of a visualisation is to determine a preferred destination. In this case, as you build a clear picture of a purpose or goal, you are also informing yourself exactly where you want to go. In other words, you are establishing a specific target. This is important because it encourages you to focus your attention and thus decreases the likelihood of falling prey to distractions. It may be suggested that the more focused your vision, the clearer your intentions and the more motivated you will be.

You may like to watch the movie *The Legend of Bagger Vance*. This story illustrates how sportspeople, in this instance golfers, use the practice of visualisation to set their future intentions. In the film, the mysterious caddie Bagger helps a troubled golfer Junuh to,

see the field.

Bagger tells Junuh everyone has their,

authentic shot.

However, as Bagger explains, too often we are so busy thinking about all of the things we are supposed to do, that we forget to notice what we are actually doing. So, Bagger counsels,

seek it with your hands,
don't think about it,
feel it.

This was sound advice. Instead of over-thinking the shot, Junuh visualises the path of his ball and feels the path it will take, and then he takes the shot. The ball falls next to the pin, and Junuh tastes the success he has been missing.

Of course, this is a movie, and as you may have noted, simply visualising an outcome does not always guarantee success. Similarly, you may have found that being motivated is often not enough.

Chapter 2: The Door

How frequently do you
set goals,
build mental pictures and
visualise yourself
achieving an outcome,

only to find the
image fades,
your concentration wanes and
you drift off course?

Why?

It may be that your motivation and visualisation lacks the fuel to be sustainable. Often motivation is powered by an external force which is beyond your immediate area of influence. If you are unable to control the motivating force, you leave yourself open to becoming a character in someone else's vision. Remember, even though you may not be able to control your environment, you can choose what you do within it. This is how you can begin to compose a *MyStory* which nestles comfortably within the *Library of Life*.

Therefore, in order to provide yourself with optimised opportunities, you need to generate your own inspiration from an internal source. Have you noticed I used the words 'yourself', 'you' and 'your'. It is important to recognise that this is an internal action. The most powerful fuel to drive your life is generated within yourself and its functionality is individualised to your unique programming. This is why the ideas or rewards which motivate one individual may not motivate another. It is also why repeating 'empty affirmations' night after night rarely yields the desired outcome. While it is true that some motivations are shared by a particular group, the most powerful ones are usually personal. In the same way, affirmations rarely have power unless they are synced internally. Let me use another story to illustrate.

In the movie *X-Men: First Class* a young Erik (Magneto) is ordered by the evil Sebastian Shaw to move a coin and save his mother. The young boy was clearly very motivated; he wanted to protect his mum. However he could not move the coin. Why? I will not spoil the film, but if you choose to watch it, you will see the catalyst for Erik's latent abilities was intensely felt emotion. While the trigger for this emotion was external, the inspiring power came from the emotional forces within. These were his specific key triggers. It is also worth noting that it was not until Erik learnt to control his emotions (and to regulate external motivators) that he gained true command of his powers. We will explore this later when we look at the power of emotions. For now, the point to note is that internal inspiration is usually significantly more powerful, and infinitely more sustainable, than external motivations.

I would like to warn you here about a common tool used in marketing. Marketing or sales professionals are often coached to highlight a pain motivation and then offer a solution. For instance, they may encourage you to feel fat so you will sign up to a particular weight loss program. While some people may lose weight, many more will put it back on after the program has finished. Worse, some may begin to believe they have a weight problem (when usually they didn't) and this develops into poor body image with disastrous psychological and physiological consequences.

From this practical example you may begin to appreciate why it is important to develop inner inspiration (and critical literacy). If a person is inspired to be the best version of themself, and this inspiration is fuelled by an inner determination to be healthy, they will perceive themselves as having the appearance of a healthy person and thus eat and exercise as a healthy person would, rather than adopting the persona of a celebrity yo-yo dieter. In this case, inner inspiration is likely to produce a more sustainable behaviour pattern than following someone else's vision of a 'thin' or 'fat' person. This is made even more powerful when a person is also able to apply critical literacy to recognise and ignore the persuasive language used by marketers. It is more powerful again, when a person learns how to sync and balance themselves (this process is explained in more detail on page 118).

By now, you may be thinking this is all very nice in theory but how do I actually develop inner inspiration? This is where the 4C model is useful. The four C's I am talking about are four internal attributes beginning with the letter 'C' – *confidence, courage, creativity* and *compassion.*

However, before we move on, have you recognised the literary technique I am using when I ask you to 4C your future? '4C' is working as a pun; a deliberate play on words (or, in this case, letter and number). Often a pun is used to engage the reader through humour or by encouraging them to actively think about the connection between concepts. In either instance the result is a more functional understanding of the ideas being presented.

So, are you actively thinking?

Can you see a connection between the concept of foresee (seeing in advance and visualising) and the relationship between four words starting with 'C' – confidence, courage, creativity and compassion?

Can you perceive a way to combine these concepts to produce the internal inspiration required to generate the future of your dreams?

Perhaps it will help to think about people such as:

- Jules Verne and Arthur C Clarke who wrote science fiction before it became science fact.
- Henry Ford and Steve Jobs who created products before consumers knew they wanted them.

• Mother Teresa and Jane Goodall who believed the world could be different and made it so.

Each of these people was inspired by a dream, a picture they saw inside their mind – by their imagination. These people were more than simple idealists, visionaries or innovators; they were 'doers' who actively took the ideas from their mind and built them into tangible realities. Of course, this took effort; it took determination, persistence and stamina. They took risks and accepted failure as nothing more than a step along the *Learning Path*. They focused resolutely on a future they could respect.

Now look at each of the C-ing characteristics and consider how they function as a collective.

Confidence　　Feeling and acting upon a sense of self-awareness, trust and security.

Courage　　Feeling and acting upon a determination to overcome fear and take action rather than procrastinate, hide or blame.

Creativity　　Feeling and acting upon a desire to generate and innovate.

Compassion　　Feeling and acting upon a genuine love, care and concern for others.

Are you beginning to realise that when the attributes of confidence, courage, creativity and compassion combine, they serve as an internally powered source of inspiration?

Imagine if you were to find within yourself each of these attributes. How would they light your *Learning Path*?

As you recognise and consolidate your ability to feel confident, courageous, creative and compassionate, you are powering an internal generator. The result is sustainable fuel. You may like to imagine confidence, courage, creativity and compassion as the attributes that can simultaneously support, guide and inform the choices you make. When you are confident in yourself and your abilities, you have the courage to accept challenges and recognise opportunities. Your feelings of security activate relationships which are interdependent and cooperative (rather than bound by ego or a compulsion to prove something). Your creativity flourishes within a flexible, adaptive attitude. You propose relevant questions and generate innovative answers. Your compassion builds peaceful, ethical and sustainable environments.

To further deepen your understanding, you may also like to reflect on how the symbolic representation of the four spiralling C's may be likened to an image of four rolling waves and how this metaphorical 'sea' represents the naturally occurring power of our own emotional and thoughtful tides.

In essence, this chapter is asking you to actively engage in your future. It is suggesting that it is possible to make a connection between the inspiration inside of you and the vision you observe in front of you. It challenges you to make a commitment to travel your *Learning Path* in a conscious manner.

Reflect

1. How can you use your understanding of the connection between 'foresee' (seeing in advance and visualising) and the four words starting with C (confidence, courage, creativity and compassion) to take responsibility for yourself?

At what point will you
choose to
4C your future.

When will you
take responsibility
for your
MyStory?

Story: The Point

'No way, man, there is no way I'm going down there. DID YOU HEAR ME, MAN! I said NO WAY!'

Desperate to merge into its solid reassurance, Lisa sank back into the rock wall behind her. She had never felt so scared. The rope in her sweaty palms felt like limp spaghetti. The harness cradling her body was as solid as cotton candy. Her heart sang a dirge while her mind screamed.

Torture.

And *he* thought she could do this?

No way! There was no way Lisa was going to put her faith in a few jumbled lines, a bright red corsetry contraption and the patient smile of a friendly guide.

No way!

'Come on Lisa, you can do this, just listen to Paul and do what he says. He'll help.' The words of her classmates, hurled from the rocky outcrop below, offered little reassurance.

'Why did I let them talk me into this?' The simple, not so high, challenge, seen from the safety of distance, morphed into a treacherously impossible chasm when observed from her current position at the edge of the cliff. 'Now I know why they say in the movies, *don't look down*,' Lisa thought miserably.

'Come on Lisa, look at the rope, it is really strong, and you have two of them.' Paul's voice was soothing and calm. 'One is anchored over there; this one is joined to me, and Jim is belaying at the base. You are well connected. I promise we won't let you fall. You control the speed. Just allow the rope to slip through there, and you hold on here.'

She could see a huddle of smiling faces encouraging her, offering support and willing her down. They genuinely wanted her to be part of this. *She* wanted to be part of this. Their words sounded so motivating. They were alluring and tempting, but still Lisa clung like a limpet to the rock behind her.

Tears welled in her eyes and her knuckles tightened around the rope Paul said would hold her. Lisa wanted to do this. She had eagerly watched as seven of her classmates inched their way down the rock face. Even her teacher was down there, and if Miss K could do it ...

'It's okay to be scared, Lisa,' Paul continued. 'This is an unnatural situation. People are not designed to go slipping down cliffs. But these ropes and this harness are. They have been designed for this purpose; to keep you safe. And they will keep you safe. But this is your decision. Think about what *you* want. Don't listen to them. Listen to me and, more importantly, listen to yourself. There is a really pretty cave down there and this section is only the first step in this adventure your teacher has organised. Once you get down onto the outcrop, you go into that hole and through a dark tunnel which winds its way deep under the earth. You will see stalactites and stalagmites, maybe even a few crystals. It is really beautiful ... but only you know if that is what you want to see. You decide. What is important to you? Why do *you* want to go down there?'

Lisa looked into Paul's kindly face. She noticed the weathered eyes watching her. She felt exposed, as though he was reaching into her soul. Unable to hold his gaze, she turned away, shaking her head.

'It's so high,' she whispered.

Again Lisa looked down to those waiting below. She looked at the mouth of the cave and then peered into herself. She wanted to see inside and more, she wanted to prove that she had the power to do what she wanted. But the only way to do that was to abseil down, and as she had recently discovered, she and heights were locked in a completely dysfunctional relationship.

So change the relationship.

'Huh?'

Change the relationship.

The words came from a forgotten space; a memory. A childhood of climbing trees and swinging on monkey bars.

'Course it's scary, but does that mean it's dangerous? You have covered the risks. You are held by ropes and you have a back-up plan. It's time to leave fear and hook up with will.

'Huh?'

Courage girl, have confidence in yourself and trust your belay. This was a voice Lisa had not heard since childhood.

Turning her head back toward Paul, she finally nodded. 'Okay, let's do this.'

Her slow and steady steps were really tiny little shuffles, but they were steps. Keeping her eyes fixed on Paul's, Lisa inched her way. The harness tightened. The rope stiffened. Lisa tensed. This was it.

She shuddered.

She stopped.

One more step and she would be off the cliff and into the air with nothing but nylon webbing and twisted hemp keeping her anchored to earth. The point of no return.

Lisa took the last step.

'Ahhhhhhhh ...' Her terrified shriek dissolved into exhalation. 'Woohooo ...'

<u>Step 3 on the *Learning Path*</u>

Discover your own place from which to write.
Settle comfortably within yourself

<u>Step</u> *1 encouraged you to peer inside yourself and
discover who you are.*

<u>Step 2</u> *asked you to 4C your future.*

Now it is time for the third step.

*Are you ready
to step inside?*

Step 3 – Discover Your Own Place from Which to Write

Whether you are taking tiny shuffles or larger strides, your next steps can take you a little deeper into your own place. Within your internal sea (pun and metaphor intended) you can find confidence, courage, creativity and compassion. From here, you may begin to sync and balance.

How?

Perhaps, before we continue, it is worth reflecting on what I mean by your own place.

Reflect

What is your first thought when I ask:

1. Where is your place?

2. Where do you feel at home?

3. What are the features within this place that make you feel at ease?

Answering these questions, or at least thinking about how you would answer them, should focus your attention on the concept of 'place'.

To clarify, when I speak of place, although I am partially referring to the physical location of your room or home (even state and country), I am also speaking about a more significant inner place. This inner place is that space within ourself that is known only to

75

ourself. You may like to imagine it as an internal multi-roomed home with your 4C generator at the centre.

Often, a connection to a particular place is intrinsically linked to our sense of who we are. This is probably why the search for connection is a common theme in young adult literature. Stories such as *Looking for Alibrandi* by Melina Marchetta illustrate how identity may be linked to a search for a place, people and culture in which to belong. Essentially a sense of connection offers a sense of security because it offers a point of attachment. The stronger this anchorage point, the greater the likelihood of developing the confident attitude, which, as you are beginning to recognise, can initiate the inspiring attributes of courage, creativity and compassion. In other words, the more connected we are, the safer we feel.

Discussions with my classes have led me to the belief that a connection to place is fundamental to feeling that we belong. Connection to place occurs when we feel accepted, valued and comfortable within a particular space. With this sense of being at ease or balanced comes the understanding that, even though challenges will arise,

> *I have a solid base (or place) from which to draw strength and achieve what I set out to achieve.*

However, if the search for connections occurs largely outside of ourself, we are at the mercy of external forces, and this can be displacing. It is disconcerting because we are relying on powers over which we have no control. In these situations, if the environment changes, we may be left without a solid anchoring place, and this can be alarming.

Therefore, we need to uncover an internal stage and inner connections; we need to learn how to sync our values and we need to learn how to centre and balance ourself. Or, in terms of the concept of belonging, we need to feel as though we belong in our own skin. When we feel connected to our inner place we are in a position to develop a sense of self-awareness and are less likely to seek external affirmations as a means to fill a perceived emptiness. Settling comfortably inside our inner place provides a feeling of being fulfilled and secure.

Imagine how relieved you will feel,
knowing that a feeling of ease,
is within your sphere of control.

Interestingly, a positive consequence of this inner security is improved outer connections and relationships. Stories such as *Looking for Alibrandi* demonstrate how the more we settle inside, the more we accept other people for who they are (rather than expecting them to conform to our belief of who they should be). We develop positive interdependent relationships rather than destructive dependencies or isolating indifferences. This occurs because we are less likely to seek external validation by arguing we are right. In other words, we are more able to acknowledge the beliefs of others while still maintaining our own values.

A useful analogy is the relationship between PC and Mac computers. As we know a PC computer can share information with a Mac, even though they both use different operating systems. Similarly, people may possess different perspectives and still communicate effectively. Of course, communication between PCs and Macs requires specialised sharing software that re-codes data allowing both systems to recognise the message. The programmers of these systems acknowledge that while individuals may prefer one operating system over the other, it is in everyone's best interest for the two systems to share common language features, especially if both systems utilise one network. People also require mutual acknowledgement of shared purpose in order to collaborate or live harmoniously. Computers use shareware, to facilitate cross-platform communication; people use compassion.

Therefore, to return to our base metaphor, recognising our place in the author's space, offers the opportunity to become self-reliant within a wider system. We become responsible because we realise we have the power to generate our own ideas, thoughts and feelings; and we know the place where these ideas, thoughts and feelings are generated. We feel comfortable coexisting within our environment because we realise the only person who can control our thoughts and emotions is ourself. Therefore, we feel safely equipped to meet environmental challenges; we know that we are cradled by our internal strengths.

This is a powerful realisation. To demonstrate in a practical sense, perhaps a brief side trip onto the friendship path is in order.

Friends are people we choose to share time with. We share ideas, feelings, hopes and dreams. Friends provide a place to be and a reason to be there. We trust our friends to keep our secrets and bolster our spirits. However, often we judge the strength of our friendship on the degree to which our friends mirror our ideas and values. Unfortunately, as reassuring as shared attitudes may be, the search for people who are 'just like me' has the potential to become complicated, especially if we don't know who we are or haven't found our inner place. If we are not secure in our identity, we may project an unstable sense of self onto our friends and thus find our own insecurities reflected back to us. Often this leads to the question:

Do my friends really know me?

Many times students have told me,

I feel lonely.
or
My friends don't seem
to understand me.

These statements are heart rending every single time. They signify a deeply felt sense of isolation. To some, acquiring more friends seems like a solid solution. However, this places power in the hands of others. Even though we want and need external connections, as you now know, if we rely on these links as our point of security, we place ourself at the mercy of variables outside our control.

A more useful strategy is to devote time to locating and becoming settled within our own place. When we feel centred and balanced inside, we are less likely to hunger for the acceptance of others in order to feel wanted and loved. We do not need to seek anchor in an external harbour; rather we float within an inner sea. We become stronger, more self-reliant and therefore more able to form valuable interdependent friendships.

The ancient philosopher Rumi suggested:

> *Your task is not to seek for love, but merely to seek and find all the barriers within yourself that you have built against it.*

In other words, in order to be a friend, we need to be a friend to ourself; we need to locate our inner place and gain an awareness of who we are. This self-awareness provides a balanced base for our 4C generator. An interesting side effect of a secure sense of self is our attractiveness to others. People seem to sense peacefulness and are drawn to its power. It seems, when you are a friend to yourself, you reflect the qualities of friendship which signals to others that you can be trusted. Put simply, rather than trying to be a friend, you are simply, friendly.

Placing the Next Step

Have you seen the movie The Matrix?

In this film the central character, Neo, is asked by Morpheus to make a choice; the red tablet or the blue. The red will return him to the life he was familiar with, the blue to a different one. Morpheus warns Neo, once he chooses, there will be no going back.

Have you read the poem 'The Road Not Taken' by Robert Frost?

In this poem the persona describes a time when he reaches a fork in the road. Accepting he can 'not travel both', he needs to make a choice and 'knowing how way leads on to way' he 'doubted if I should ever come back.'

Can you remember how Lisa felt in the short story, 'The Point'?

In this short story, Lisa stood at the top of the cliff and realised she had a choice; she could remain where she was, or explore the cave below. She understood that once she stepped off the cliff, she would not return to the point she was leaving.

This is the point of no return and, when faced with this place, Lisa experienced terror, Neo felt anxious and Frost's persona acknowledged regret, yet each chose to act. Each decided they wanted to see the place on the path ahead.

How do you feel right now?

Are you ready to
place the next step?

Do you want to locate

your inner place?

The Place Ahead – Recognise your Strengths

The initial chapters of *MyStory* encouraged you to actively read and reflect on the ideas presented. Have you been asking questions and challenging the concepts? Did you complete the exercises?

Remember these questions and tasks were designed to help you recognise your authentic self and build your stamina or mindset. However, even though these responses provide fuel for your quest along the *Learning Path*, as you have learnt, sustained power comes from within. Therefore it is time to locate your inner place and 4C generator.

Essentially your inner place and 4C generator is a figurative expression for your innate strengths and core values. Therefore recognising and celebrating your strengths is one way to locate your inner power reserves (we will look at core values in the next chapter). As I have said countless times already, the more aware of who you are, the more secure and comfortable you are likely to feel and the easier the *Learning Path* will seem. An example should reinforce this message.

Imagine walking into your History classroom and being told you have a Maths test.

- You probably feel disorientated – you were expecting to learn History, not Maths.
- You probably feel anxious – you were not aware you were going to have a test and did not prepare.
- You probably feel frustrated – you wonder how you could possibly pass a test you were not told about.

Now imagine a second scenario. This time you are told you will have a Maths test in three days' time, in your regular Maths classroom.

- You are given a detailed outline of what will be on the test.

- You are given revision notes and practice questions.
- At home, you carefully revise the study notes and complete the practice exercises.
- At school you speak to your teacher to clarify any material you did not understand.

Now how do you feel as you walk into the test? You probably feel reasonably confident. Even if there are some challenging questions on the paper, you are likely to adopt a courageous approach because you know the required formulas and feel comfortable with your preparation.

Therefore, being aware, knowing what to expect and recognising your strengths, builds confidence. When you recognise your strengths and gather them together, you realise that you have the tools or capacity to survive. This fosters courage and creativity while still leaving space for compassion.

How Do You Begin to Recognise Your Strengths?

You may like to begin by actually defining and identifying the characteristics that represent strength. Then you can recognise strengths in others and highlight the strengths you value. This establishes a context for you to acknowledge your own strengths. This process draws on the concepts of 'projection' and 'authentic self'[3]

The concept of projection in psychological terms, refers to a person's tendency to project their own thoughts and feelings on to another person rather than addressing the thought or feeling themself. This is what I was referring to earlier when I suggested people with a shifting sense of identity may transfer those feelings onto their friends, leading to the belief that their friends do not

---

[3] I only offer a very brief, simplistic explanation of these concepts here, however you may like to conduct your own research and use the critical evaluation technique GRASP, to gain a more detailed understanding.

understand them when, in reality, it may be that they do not understand themself.

The concept of authentic self in psychological and philosophical terms may be simply understood as our balanced and centred self, or the recognised and acknowledged 'inner me'. (We will explore this concept a little further when we look at core values in the next chapter.)

Combining the concepts of projection and authentic self, it is possible to suggest that the qualities we admire in another person are the qualities we would like to have in ourself. If we hold this as true, and we accept that our authentic self guides us toward who we really are, it is probable that the strengths we value in others also exist inside us; even if we have yet to consciously acknowledge them.

What is a Personal Strength?

You may like to think of a personal strength as a character trait or attitude that enables you to achieve a desired outcome. In this regard, your strengths become your facilitating qualities; they are the power source behind your actions.

Although a quick tap of keys will yield a multitude of websites that list strengths and offer questionnaires, be cautious. These tests are interesting and may offer clues about your key strengths. Nevertheless they are simply an impression of you, they are not actually you. If you take these tests, remember to apply critical evaluation strategies and reflect upon what they say rather than accepting them as actual truth. In other words, use them to gain a greater understanding of yourself, not to tell you who you are.

Actually, this advice holds true for any form of 'who am I' questionnaire. Many psychometric tests aim to classify and measure personality types and responses. Have you ever taken such a test and noticed that some of the questions were difficult to answer because they did not seem applicable to you or your situation? What did this suggest to you? It should have suggested that standardised tests are not personally relevant for every individual on the planet. These tests process data and offer statistically reasoned opinion. Therefore the data is not 100 per cent reliable; it is simply a guide. While the results may be informative, the true value of these tests lie in the opportunity they provide to GRASP (see page 21) an impression of yourself. If you take one of these tests, your intention should be to uncover a fresh perspective and alert your consciousness to patterns of behaviour or ideas that you may not have noticed. It should not be a way to neatly categorise yourself into a 'type'.

This is why the questions below ask you to think about your interpretations. There are no right or wrong answers. These questions encourage you to reflect upon your impression of the character traits of survivors. The objective is to open your mind to the extraordinary things that ordinary people can do. At the same time, as you think about the qualities you value in others, you may begin to gain an insight into the powerful characteristics within you.

Reflect

1. Think about a movie or book that explores a survival situation (e.g. The 'Transformers' movie series or *Tomorrow When the War Began* by John Marsden or even, *Lord of the Flies* by William Golding).

   a. Identify the event that places the characters in danger.

   b. Was the danger physical or psychological, or a combination of both?

c. What strategies were used to survive?

d. Which character do you most identify with?

e. How would you react in a similar situation?

2. Consider the list of survival characteristics below and rate them from 1 – 12 where 1 is the most valuable survival trait and 12 is the least.

☐ Love	☐ Loyalty	☐ Ingenuity
☐ Hope	☐ Determination	☐ Persistence
☐ Faith	☐ Flexibility	☐ Strong: physical
☐ Optimism	☐ Bravery	☐ Strong: emotional

Look carefully at your top five. Can you make any connections between these and your responses to the previous question?

Approach

Write Carefully consider your responses to the **Reflect** questions. Use them to write a reflective journal (or blog) that explores your perception of survival.

By now you should be
gaining a greater understanding
of personal strengths and be
recognising the ones
you value most.

The next set of exercises asks you to focus
on the strengths you see in you.

Reflect

1. Consider the list of strengths below and choose five that you think relate to you. Record them on a separate sheet of paper or in a journal.

2. Show the list of strengths below to a friend and ask them to point out five strengths they admire in you. Record them on a separate sheet of paper.

3. Show the list of strengths below to a parent or teacher and ask them to point out five strengths they admire in you. Record them on a separate sheet of paper.

1. flexible	18. forgiving	35. proactive
2. adventurous	19. friendly	36. generous
3. confident	20. honest	37. loyal
4. accomplished	21. loving	38. attentive
5. compassionate	22. funny	39. innovative
6. leadership	23. relaxed	40. exciting
7. attentive	24. sensitive	41. considerate
8. content	25. reflective	42. optimistic
9. happy	26. patient	43. spiritual
10. competent	27. independent	44. originality
11. harmonious	28. faithful	45. focused
12 purposeful	29. consistent	46. positive
13. team player	30. imaginative	47. innovative
14. creative	31. responsible	48. peaceful
15. courageous	32. resourceful	49. persistent
16. determined	33. decisive	50. cooperative
17. faith	34. practical	

What do the selections made by yourself, your friend and your parents suggest about you and the way you present yourself to other people? Do you present the image you want to convey?

Approach

Write: Consider your current feelings and thoughts. What you have learnt from this exercise? Write in your journal or blog.

Your Strength

Focus on the strengths you value and they are likely to assume a more tangible form. As they take shape in your consciousness you will become better equipped to use them; you will feel the power in your hands or the keys at your fingertips. In essence this means you have entered the place of choice, a place where you can choose to begin writing your *MyStory*. From this position you may chose to focus on what you can do, rather than what you cannot do.

This concept is aptly portrayed in the movie *The Empire Strikes Back* (from the 'Star Wars' film series). While training Luke to use the skills of a Jedi Knight, Yoda explains,

'Do ... or do not. There is no try.'

Luke feels frustrated by the apparent loss of his X-wing fighter and is sceptical of Yoda's belief that it could be reclaimed. If you watch this scene you will notice the difference between the strength of a *can do* attitude, as opposed to the weaker, *I can try*.

However this scene also highlights how individual strengths may be enhanced by recognising how the individual is part of a wider system. Earlier in this swamp scene, Yoda explains the concept of The Force (which seems similar to the bio-botanical connections fuelled by the Tree of Souls in the movie *Avatar*). Both *The Empire Strikes Back* and *Avatar* encourage audiences to become aware of a wider energy that exists beyond what can be seen. These stories offer an illustration of how individuals exist as part of a wider system. Similarly, as mentioned earlier, PC and Mac computers use shared software to function comfortably within a single network. Therefore, even though you are being encouraged to write your own story, your story has a place within a larger library.

Chapter 2: The Door

In order to function comfortably people also need to recognise their position within a wider system.

Throughout this chapter I have referred to a need to centre and balance yourself. This process is easier when we locate our internal or moral compass. These values and ethics form a guidance system which can help you forge connections that are congruent to your authentic self. They provide a solid stage from which to navigate the *Learning Path*.

First you needed to understand your inner world.

Now it is time to recognise
how your inner world connects
to the outer environment.

Story: The Rite II

Darkness unfurled its wings and embraced the world driving piercing cold into every pore.

Tania knew it was time to stop. Although she was desperate to push forward, she understood now was not the time. This was an opportunity to rest, regroup and ensure she was prepared for the greater challenge that lay ahead.

But she didn't want to stop. She wanted to see what was over the next hill. It was just a little further. Tania was convinced it would be a better place than where she was now. Surely it wouldn't hurt to ...

No. Perhaps this is where the others failed. Maybe they were lured into the abyss. Maybe the sirens' song cajoled them with the heated excitement of false hope.

Closing her thoughts to the distant allure, Tania reached inside her knapsack. It held her tools. Resting comfortably, trusting her preparation, Tania felt for the supplies she had packed the morning before.

Fire was her first priority. It would keep the dark cold at bay. Next she needed to build a shelter, a base to protect herself from the elements. Then she could eat and refuel her tired body. Steps, a plan, a clear strategy – this thought brought relief and hope.

She could do this.

Firewood was easy to find. It lay scattered like abandoned toys waiting to be collected. Within minutes Tania had gathered a sizable stack. With deft movements, she struck the flint and lit the fire. Pausing for a moment she allowed the warmth to penetrate through to her aching muscles.

I can do this.

The tall, wise oak stood guard. It had maintained this position for centuries. Growing, renewing. Solid and trustworthy, the tree welcomed Tania with outstretched limbs, offering to share its space. Gratefully, she flung her spare skins over a low-hanging branch and secured them with the ropes she had brought from home.

I am doing this.

The fire crackled contentedly as Tania fed it a few solid logs. These larger pieces of timber would burn slowly, providing sustained heat. Sitting comfortably inside the shelter, with the fire burning close by, Tania reached into her bag for the carefully wrapped food. Although the meat was tough, it was tasty and nourishing. She watched the dancing flames project filament shapes on the walls of her tiny cocoon. They seemed strong, flexible, and determined in their movements; ingeniously they swayed in balanced harmony as if following a secret rhythmic beat. Tania knew they were only shadows, but in the darkness they provided hope. Sated by the food and warmth, she breathed deeply and allowed her thoughts to settle before sleep claimed her.

The morning sun prodded Tania awake. Glaring brightly, it tickled and teased until she opened her eyes to survey the newly created day.

I have done this.

Confidently she rolled up the shelter and neatly repacked it into the knapsack. Pausing only briefly to nibble on another strip of dried meat, Tania readied herself to continue her Rite. Renewed and revitalised she felt grateful for the insight and patience that had prompted her to rest in this place. Shouldering her bag she reached down to gather the bow she had left at the base of the tree. An acorn lay by its side. Picking it up Tania marvelled at the ingenuity of nature. This tiny seed stored the tools the future oak would need. From this small nut, life would grow.

<u>Step 4 on the *Learning Path*</u>

Navigate with your *Honour Compass*
Sync and balance

<u>*Step 1*</u> *encouraged you to peer inside yourself and discover who you are.*

<u>*Step 2*</u> *asked you to 4C your future.*

<u>*Step 3*</u> *proposed the discovery of your own place.*

Now it is time for the fourth step.

*Will you choose to
dance in harmony
or rage in dispute?*

Step 4: Navigate with Your *Honour Compass*

As you completed the previous <u>Reflect</u> and <u>Approach</u> sections you were locating your inner place and 4C generator. However, to feel truly comfortable within yourself, you need to recognise that you are part of a larger social system. This recognition of symbiotic relationships positions you within a greater energy field. Remember, even though sustained energy is internally powered, we live in the world and are exposed to external forces. Our own story is embedded within a larger library and our systems programs operate within a complex network. Therefore we need a guidance tool that will help us navigate the *Learning Path*. We need to recognise our innate core values; the morals and ethics which regulate our behaviour. We need a strategy that offers synchronicity within a wider system.

Motivational speakers may attempt to excite you with claims of:

- You can be whatever you want to be.

- You can do whatever you want to do.

- Simply think it and you can do it.

While these statements may be encouraging, by now you know affirmations are empty without inner inspiration. Platitudes such as these are powerless, unless you make the choice to achieve and the fuel powering your choice is inwardly inspired.

Your 4C generator can provide energy; it supplies the confidence, courage, creativity and compassion necessary to put thought into action. However, there is a caveat to the 'you can do anything you want' sentiment – your authentic self, your higher self, your moral self, needs to agree with you. In other words, your actions are more likely to be effective, your behaviour constructive, your emotions assured, when they are aligned to your core values. This is what I have been referring to when I suggest the need to sync and balance. The aim of this chapter is to offer a map to your authentic self. Figuratively speaking, this is the core aspect of your internal beliefs. It is your *Honour Compass*.

This concept of honour and authentic self was aptly explored in the movie *A Knight's Tale*. I confess, this movie is one of my all-time favourites. Watch it mindfully and the message is clear,

we can change our stars.

In the movie, William, the son of a common thatcher deliberately seizes the opportunity to create the life of his dreams – the life of a knight. Throughout the film, audiences learn that despite his peasant birth, William has the character traits of a noble; in fact, he is more honourable than those of noble birth. This is the key to William's success. He is a knight in his heart and lives according to his principles, even if it means being unfairly judged. If you view the film, pay close attention to the final section of the movie. I will not spoil anything here; suffice to say it illustrates the concept of choosing your own destiny by following your core values.

Approach

View   Watch this movie. It will consolidate much of the learnings you have collected thus far.

Choice and Honour

Identifying your ideals, standards and principles is important because these form the core values of your honour code. The guidance they offer becomes particularly relevant when making choices about your future. For instance, an awareness of what has personal significance for you may lead to a decision to delay gratification today, so that you may gain greater rewards tomorrow. Similarly, understanding what has meaning for you, may encourage the confidence and compassion required to build symbiotic relationships. Recognition of your honour code can provide a state of inner harmony which places you in a position to write your *MyStory* in a way that enriches networks, rather than draining them.

In his book *The 7 Habits of Highly Effective People*[4] Stephen Covey devotes numerous chapters to explaining how awareness of, and aligning to, core values facilitates interdependent relationships. In simple summary, he suggests that harmonious relationships are possible when we understand the difference between our needs (values) and wants (desires) and let go of any attachments which are not synchronised to our principles. This behavioural and attitudinal choice enables an individual to act honourably and live a life of integrity.

Remember, just as you have a choice in what you do (or say) today, you have a choice in the inheritance you offer the future. You live in a wider system and your actions have an impact on those around you. Your story is housed in *The Library of Life*.

Have you ever heard the expression:

Your choices have consequences?

---

[4] Stephen Covey, *The 7 Habits of Highly Effective People*, Business Library, Melbourne, 1995 ed.

What does this expression mean to you and how do you respond when you hear it? Are you able to recognise the difference between wants and needs; when to let go and when to push forward? Can you identify the difference between actions, thoughts and behaviours based on needs and those fuelled by desire?

Although the movie *Never Back Down* is a little too violent for my tastes, it does illustrate the notion of choosing which battles to fight based on an understanding of your values. In the beginning of the movie Jake claims he feels

angry all the time.

He fights external battles in an effort to mask the internal conflict raging inside. However, as he learns about himself and recognises his moral code, he realises the difference between the battles which are important and those which were driven by self doubt.

Before I continue I should point out that I am not talking about giving in or giving up. I am talking about letting go of what is not in harmony with your values. This is demonstrated in *Never Back Down* when Jake explains to his coach, Roqua,

Doing nothing has consequences too ...
this is my fight and everyone has one.

In other words each individual has the ability to reflect on a situation, find their centre and then balance and synchronise their values with possible outcomes, before they choose a response.

Of course to do this, you need to know the difference between what is important and what is not. You need to become aware of your values and honour code. Often behavioural choices are based on how the action will be perceived by others (or to gain attention) rather than what is in harmony with internal values. Therefore, it is important to learn how to distinguish between the true voice of your authentic self and the mindless chatter of self doubt. This allows you to act, rather than react.

One way to determine the validity of a particular response is to ask yourself, will this action be in tune with my beliefs.

Will it
create a harmonious melody,
or
a screeching discord?

Sometimes, you will find a compromise. Different instruments can work cooperatively to form rhythmic patterns. However, at other times you may need to choose one way or another; to beat the drum, rather than strum the harp. In either case, when faced with options, if you are aware of your own honour code and can trust your inner compass, you will be in a better position to make an authentic decision. An authentic decision is one which promotes social synchronicity and is in accord with your authentic self. This can lead to an inner balance that promulgates outer peace.

Another movie illustration is housed within *The Karate Kid*, both the original 1984 version and the 2010 remake. Both Mr Miyagi and Mr Han counsel their students to find a place of inner balance, a place of stability from which to draw energy. They explain to Daniel and Dre that resistance is a damaging force that drains energy. Emotions such as fear, anger, jealousy and greed are examples of resistance forces which are often formed by our perception of other people's expectations. If we feel powerless or unworthy of meeting an expectation, these emotions create disharmony. Other times an expectation may be completely out of alignment with a core value leading to an internal conflict where the authentic self wrestles with self doubt. However, as Daniel and Dre discover, when we simply let go of expectations, and instead focus on the present and align our values, we can access an internal energy flow. Put simply if we allow rather than resist we may find harmony.

Can you imagine how it will feel
when you access your values and
live in your present?

Will you choose to locate your
Honour Compass?

Locating your Honour Compass

Earlier I spoke about finding a secure anchorage point within yourself. This is the protected place to which you may return when the sea outside is rough. It is the place that offers inner support when the outer world is besieged by storms. The stage you stand on when making a choice that will satisfy both the personal audience and public connections. A place where you feel centred and balanced.

In order to access this centred stage, you need to uncover your innate guidance system. This guidance system is the product of your authentic self and an understanding of your role within a wider system. I have been encouraging you to imagine this as an inner compass and, just as a compass relies on detecting the earth's magnetic pull, an *Honour Compass* functions by detecting your core values. It acts as a balancing force between your authentic self and the outer appearances of personality.

Before continuing it may be useful to clarify the terms: values, morals and ethics.

Values

Values may be defined as the attributes, attitudes and ideas that have particular significance or worth. Social values are those behaviours and ideals which are socially important because they are perceived as being correct or just within society. Similarly, personal values are those actions and thoughts which have particular worth and importance to the individual.

Although social and personal values are similar, the hierarchy of particular values may vary from individual to individual, individual to culture and culture to culture. For instance, one person may place love and hope as their core values, whereas their culture may assign higher values to justice and loyalty.

It is useful to reflect on your values (and from where they are derived) since, in most cases, your values moderate and dictate your actions.

Morals

It may be suggested that morals are the principles or rules used by individuals or cultures to choose a correct pattern of behaviour. In most cases, these are based on the values which are believed to evoke cooperative effort. Therefore morals usually recognise a need for protection, fairness and equity.

Ethics

Essentially ethics and morals are similar; both terms describe the standards used by individuals or groups to choose behavioural patterns. However, I like to think of ethics as the first filter for determining if a particular behaviour is in accordance with my morals and values. Generally, ethics may be a little more situational or group dependant, whereas morals tend to be firmly fixed to our personal values.

Into the Looking Glass

One of the roles of a teacher or mentor is to 'hold the mirror'. We do this so that students can see what they are doing and learn from their own actions.

Picture the dancer who practises in a mirrored studio.

Think about the football team whose games are videoed and played back during training sessions.

These examples illustrate that learning is more than simply acquiring an ability to do something or obtain information. Learning requires noticing and recognising who we are, what we are doing and then adapting to meet a preferred outcome. Learning, like life, is a dynamic process of change and choices.

Following in the footsteps of the dancer and footballer you can monitor your movements, distinguish your mindset and become aware of your emotional state. This vision and flexibility can help you write your *MyStory*, rather than being caught in someone else's.

Now, as I hold up the mirror, look into it. Open the door to your mind and gaze within to uncover your core values.

Are you ready to answer questions
that can help you learn about
your values, morals and ethics?

Reflect

1. How would you define the terms:

   - Respect

   - Faithfulness

   - Integrity

   - Loyalty

   - Fairness

   - Responsibility

   - Reliability

   - Honesty

   - Love

   - Hope

2. Rate the above feelings and attitudes (1 – 10). Would you add any other attributes which are not mentioned above?

3. Think about your relationships with friends and family. How important are the above feelings and attitudes?

Approach

Your objective in this section is to delve within and uncover your values. Decide what is really important to you. This personal pursuit deserves serious, sincere attention, so complete these exercises when you are genuinely willing to devote yourself to the task. This is your value-seeking mission.

Think Who and what is important to you? Why?

What has special significance (value) for you?

What are you grateful for?

How do you expect others to behave toward you?

Discover   Imagine a genie appearing before you and offering you three wishes. What do you wish for?

i) Write down your first wish.

ii) Then, ask the question 'for what purpose?' (e.g. I wish ... for the purpose of ...)

iii) Write down your answer.

iv) Then ask the question again (I wish ... for the purpose of ... which is for the purpose of ...)

v) Keep asking the question until you reach your value. (I wish ... for the purpose of ... which is for the purpose of ... which is for the purpose of ... which is for the purpose of ... because I value ...)

First wish

I wish _____

for the purpose of _____
_____

for the purpose of _____
_____

for the purpose of _____
_____

for the purpose of _____
_____

because I value _____

Second wish

    I wish _____

    for the purpose of _____
                        _____

    for the purpose of _____
                        _____

    for the purpose of _____
                        _____

    for the purpose of _____
                        _____

    because I value _____

Third wish

    I wish _____

    for the purpose of _____
                        _____

    for the purpose of _____
                        _____

    for the purpose of _____
                        _____

    for the purpose of _____
                        _____

    because I value _____

Synthesise

Look at your previous responses to the think and discover questions. Use your responses to write a core vision of yourself. This is a reflection of your *Honour Compass*.

I have included both a scaffold and blank lines; choose to write your response where you feel most comfortable.

I live a life of _____

I believe_____

and value_____

My relationships are _____

because I_____

or

_____

_____

_____

_____

_____

Story: A Simple Call

'You do it.'

'No you.'

'It's your house.'

'It's your idea.'

Delicious excitement flushed their cheeks while adrenaline flooded their veins. Two pairs of wide eyes; a silent dare to continue the crime. It was wrong, of course they knew it was wrong ... but it was only a *little* wrong. A harmless prank. No-one would know and no-one would get hurt. A simple phone call.

'Oh all right, I'll speak,' Lisa capitulated. 'If you dial the number.'

Picking up the phone she turned it to face Mary who slowly tapped the numbers.

One ring, two rings, three rings, four ... just as Lisa was ready to hang up with a relieved sigh, she heard a tentative voice.

'Hello ... Hello ... who is this?'

Barely containing a guilty giggle, Lisa spoke, 'Oh, hi ... um ... this is Jane, I'm a friend of Oliver's ... a friend from school, is he home, can I speak with him?'

'Jane, from ... from school was it?' The puzzled voice turned cautious. 'Is ... is this about homework?'

'Not really, I just wanted to tell him ... that ... um ... I ...' Lisa stifled a giggle.

In the background she heard an eager voice sing out, 'Mum, Mum, is that for me?'

A fumbling sound followed and then a breathless 'Hel ... hel ... hello' as a shy, somewhat perplexed Oliver took the phone from his mother.

'Hey Oliver, this is Jane, you know ... from school.'

'Um yes, wh ... wh ... why are you calling?'

'Well, I think you are such a hunk and so cute and I really wanna go out with you. I wanna kiss you and ...'

Unable to contain her mirth, Mary had started to giggle. It was contagious. Lisa sent waves of laughter down the phone, drowning Oliver in confusion.

Click.

The line went dead.

Mary and Lisa continued to laugh.

* * * * * *

The recess bell brought its customary relief. Students streamed out of confining classrooms, spilling onto the playground in pursuit of food and entertainment.

'Hey, did you hear about Oliver?'

'Yeah, some chick called him last night.'

'Oliver ... no way ... no-one calls him.'

'Well somebody did.'

'His mum musta lost it. Isn't she like ... really strict and expecting him to like ... study all the time.'

'That's what I heard ... he's not even allowed to have a girlfriend until he is like 30 or something.'

Chapter 2: The Door

'Heh heh ... I woulda loved to have heard what went on in his house last night.'

Lisa and Mary exchanged secret smiles. This felt amazing. Everyone was talking about something they did ... of course no-one knew it was them, but even anonymous fame felt wickedly satisfying. Oliver wouldn't mind, look at how everyone was talking about him – poor guy, he had never had this much attention. People may even start to recognise him. He must be feeling really special.

'Apparently this chick said she wanted to be his girlfriend ... The guy has no clue ...'

'Whatcha mean?'

'Well ... he thought it was Jane, so he spoke to her. You know how Jane is ... she just looked straight through him and asked, who the hell are you?'

'The guy was shattered.'

'Apparently his mum grounded him. She thinks he has been sneaking off to be with girls when he told her he was studying in the library.'

'But that dude is always in the library!'

'I know ... that's what makes it so funny.'

A slight figure pushed past, a shield of books hugged tightly against his chest.

Oliver.

As Lisa and Mary turned their attention away from the chatter of other students they watched Oliver slide across the playground. Head bowed, shoulders hunched he furtively moved towards a forgotten corner of the oval. They exchanged glances. Oliver didn't look like someone who was enjoying the notoriety.

'What a loser.'

'Dumbass.'

The other students had noticed Oliver.

The feelings coursing through Lisa and Mary no longer felt so good. In silent agreement they walked towards the forgotten corner of the oval.

Choosing to Use Your Compass

Have you ever wondered why people act meanly or tease, and find it amusing? Why did Lisa and Mary call Oliver? Why do radio stations make prank calls, humiliating people for humorous effect?

Is it because kindness and respect
are not regarded as significant values,

or

is it simply a way to mask internal fears of
'not enough'?

Have you noticed that sometimes, in a quest to de-stress our own experience, or to find popularity, we project our anxiety, insecurity and pressures on to others. We may be tempted to put others down or blame them for the feelings we are experiencing.

However, as the movie *Dangerous Minds* demonstrates, we have options. Teacher Lou-Anne Johnson informs her class,

'You have a choice. You can stay or leave.'

When the class challenges this idea, claiming they needed to be in class in order to graduate, she retorts,

'It may not be a choice you like, but it is a choice.'

According to Dr William Glasser's *Choice Theory*[5], people make choices in an attempt to find:

- love
- belonging
- power
- freedom
- fun
- survival

In other words choices are made to fulfil a need or desire. However, what happens when an individual perceives there is a shortage of something they need or desire? One analogy I like to use with my classes involves a chocolate bar.

First I ask the class to pretend there is one bar of chocolate on the desk and there are 20 of us. I ask how (and if) the chocolate should be shared. Invariably the perceived scarcity of the resource and the suspected competition for it produces feelings of inequity, frustration, anxiety and, sometimes, anger. The students raise objections fearing they will either miss out on a share of the chocolate or they will receive such a tiny piece that it is hardly worth dividing. Some choose to give it all away so no-one has any.

When I ask them to reflect on their answers and what prompted their responses, I query why no-one questioned if more chocolate was available. I ask them to consider if their feelings would change if I told them there were hundreds of chocolate bars in the cupboard, and that gaining access simply required them to open the door and reach inside.

I think by now you can see where I am going with this. Suffice to say, when we become aware of the limitless access we have

---

[5] William Glasser Institute, www.wglasser.com

to internal resources, we are less fearful of not enough and may begin to appreciate the wealth of opportunities surrounding us.

Hopefully you are beginning to realise that you have choices. Even though you may not always like the options in front of you, essentially, you still have a choice. When you are internally inspired, your 4C generator can provide the fuel to maintain your place on the *Learning Path* so you can focus on your chosen destination. Remember your behaviour is the result of the choices you make in response to your perceived needs, your thoughts and your feelings. You can reflect on the value of your needs. You can become conscious of your thoughts and emotions in relation to those values and needs. Although it may be difficult to choose emotions, you can choose your response to them. You can choose which ones to pay attention to and which ones to let go. You can choose to be guided from the inside, rather than directed by external fears.

You decide: is popularity more important than kindness, is pride more important than faithfulness, is pity more important than respect?

Covey writes, 'between stimulus and response man has the freedom to choose'.[6] In essence this concept is at the heart of *MyStory*. The whole metaphor is built around the principle of choice, we can choose to write our own *MyStory*, rather than being a character in someone else's. Even though we may not be able to control our environment, we can decide what we do within it. When choices are guided by our *Honour Compass* we begin to distinguish our emotions and thoughts. Therefore we are more likely to find the space to act, rather than react.

Have you ever reacted and felt the discontent
that arose from resisting your authentic self?

---

[6] Stephen Covey, *The 7 Habits of Highly Effective People*, Business Library, Melbourne, 1995 ed. pp. 70

Is This *MyStory*

Would you rather
use your Honour Compass,
allow what follows,
and feel content?

The tools we require have been given to us, but we need to recognise and identify them and then make the choice to use them. I like to call this process, 'syncing' and 'balancing'.

Syncing and Balancing

You may have been wondering when I would get around to explaining this abstract concept in more tangible form. By now, I hope you are gaining greater awareness of who you are and what you value. I hope you are learning how to access your systems programs. So far this chapter has focused on:

- Describing an *Honour Compass*.
- Illustrating how an *Honour Compass* is used.
- Giving you some strategies to locate your *Honour Compass*.
- Using your *Honour Compass* when making a choice.

Now a computer metaphor can help illustrate the concept of syncing and balancing. This process has a dual function. Used one way, it can help you find a stable foundation which synchronises you with the outside world; used another, it helps maintain inner harmony.

Before continuing, please remember this is a metaphor, not an exact replica of a situation. So use your imagination to understand the concept rather than being bogged down with specific details or potential inaccuracies.

Earlier I mentioned the differences between Mac and PC computers and explained how, even though they run different system software, they can function on a single network. Now I would like you to imagine a network with many different computers, various brands and multiple models. Each of the computers has their own hard drive and operating system. In order to connect to the other computers on the network, they require shared networking software. At regular intervals each individual computer needs to synchronise to the main server so that the data is backed up in a central location.

A similar process exists between an iPod, a computer and iTunes. When an iPod is linked using a USB cable to a computer, the iPod can 'choose' which songs to sync through the iTunes software.

As people, we are both the individual computer within a larger network needing shareware to function efficiently on a larger platform and the iPod which shares the software but can choose which songs to carry inside.

Stay with me, even if this is not altogether clear; essentially, this metaphor is an attempt to illustrate our individuality within a community.

Think about it this way: we process information through our own set of filters (or programs). We use our own understandings and perceptions to make judgements about what we see, hear and feel. Just as an individual computer on a network does not compare its data processing to other computers, we probably take the internal workings of our brain for granted. After all, we have only ever been inside our own head. Even though movies such as *Freaky Friday* explore what happens when a mother and daughter trade bodies, it would be very difficult to trade minds and still be consciously aware of the mind you left behind.

Of course we can be empathetic and imagine how another person may feel or think and we can even hypothesise why they feel or think that way. We can study the brain and its functions and we can interview, counsel and examine people's reactions to various stimuli. We can listen to or read their opinions and beliefs. We can

119

hear an explanation of their thought processes. We can watch or have their emotional responses described to us. Yet, we will still compute the information using our own operating systems. So we have no way (at least to my knowledge) of really knowing how compatible our systems are. Can we ever really know precisely what another person is thinking or feeling?

This is where the concept of shared software is applicable. In other words, in order for individuals to live within a system (or society) there must be a series of shared and accepted, behavioural patterns. These patterns recognise an individual's accountability for their actions as well as a responsibility to respect the emotional, intellectual and physical safety of others. Therefore we need to synchronise our values to the society or community in which we live. As individuals (iPods) we choose the values (songs) from the shared software and we sync them to our authentic self (internal system program).

I believe an individual who recognises their position as a synergised component in a wider system is more likely to accept the unique thoughts of others. This idea is eloquently expressed by the philosopher Rumi who proposed,

Out beyond ideas
of wrong doing and right doing
there is a field.
I'll meet you there.

To explore this concept a little further, think about a time when someone did not agree with you. Did you feel the need to prove you were right? Have you ever wondered why you felt this way? How satisfied were you with your emotional response at the time? Was it a pleasant emotion?

It may be suggested that the more you are externally synced and internally balanced, the more secure you will feel within yourself and the less likely to feel anxious, frustrated or rejected if others do not share your opinion. In other words, you may not feel as though you have something to prove and therefore may not argue or act aggressively. Rather, you may choose to recognise a simple difference of opinion, manage your responses and behave assertively or cooperatively. Therefore, syncing and balancing enables you to become more consciously aware of the choices you make when interacting with others. As a result, you are able to write a *MyStory* which nestles comfortably within the *Library of Life*.

A Note about Role Models and Mentors

Before we continue along the *Learning Path*, it is worth making brief mention of role models and mentors. These are the people who can offer an external hub or 'USB connecting cord' for syncing and balancing. As a loose definition:

- A role model is a person we admire; we would literally like to model their behaviour.
- A mentor is a person who acts as guide and counsellor for a particular aspect of our life.

As movies such as *The Karate Kid*, and *Never Back Down* demonstrate, role models, mentors and coaches may have a profound impact on a young person's life. They can offer support and guidance and they can hold a mirror so that a person may see themself from different perspectives. They can provide encouragement and direction.

When you are in the company of a person (or people) you want to emulate, you have the opportunity to learn and experience the constructive behavioural patterns which will help you achieve purpose and reach your desired destination.

However, it is important to choose appropriately. Even though sportspeople and celebrities may be popular choices as role models or mentors, perhaps they shouldn't be. It is worth noting that just because a person may be successful at their sport, or skilful in a particular area, it does not mean they have the personal qualities you want emulate – they can teach you about sport, but that does not necessarily mean they can teach you about being a good person.

This is another reason why it is important to uncover your *Honour Compass*, it can help you locate role models or mentors who are compatible with who you really are and what you truly want to achieve.

Having contact with a mentor who has already achieved success in your chosen field, or who has demonstrated the qualities of character you admire, can be of great comfort. So take the time to look carefully at the people in your life; you may have an aunt, uncle, teacher, coach, peer support person, or even a colleague or manager at work, who could act in a mentor capacity. They could be a trusted guide or advisor. A person with whom you can discuss ideas and someone who can listen with an understanding ear. Remember a mentor must be chosen very carefully. It is vital that they exhibit qualities which harmonise with your authentic self.

At this point it is also worth noting that a person may be a role model even if you do not personally know them. For instance, it is possible to read autobiographies and research the achievements of a person you admire. Reading or watching documentaries about the steps other people took to achieve their goals can be both instructive and motivating. Also remember, it is possible to have different role models for different aspects of your life. For example you may admire one person for their sports ability, another for their business acumen and a different person for their concern for others.

In this way it is possible to shape an imaginary board of directors with yourself as chairman. On this imaginary board, you retain the power to choose the direction of your life; however you may take counsel from the advisors you have selected. Even though you do not personally know or see these multiple role models, you can imagine their response to a particular situation. Then you can synthesise multiple perspectives and propose an alternate response which draws upon *your* values and their experience.

Reflect

1. Who do you admire?

2. Why do you admire them?

3. What qualities does this person have that you would like to emulate?

4. To what extent do these qualities correspond with your values?

5. What could you learn from this person that would help you with a specific aspect of your life?

How do you feel at this moment?
What are you thinking right now?

Can you see how your thoughts and emotions
are in a symbiotic relationship with your
core values and
that these may guide your actions?

Have you noticed how your
values, thoughts and emotions
influence your actions?

Will awareness of your *Honour Compass*
provide you with the direction and understanding
that your choices are yours
and you are responsible for them?

Are you becoming aware of
your position as the author?

Are you ready to climb onto the stage?
and *GRASP* your technique.

Chapter 3

The STAGE

Within the World of Expression

MyStory Technique

Develop Your *MyStory* Technique

In the previous chapter, you were encouraged to identify yourself as the author; to pass through the door and climb down into the inner realm. This involved becoming aware of who you perceive yourself to be, locating your internal power source and uncovering the values which guide you. These steps led you to this stage.

As you wander through the next pages, you will be encouraged to adopt a balanced stance upon this stage. You may like to imagine this as your control centre and it is from here that you use your *Honour Compass* to plot the course on your *Learning Path*. It also provides the platform for your 4C generator.

Your learning objective is to develop awareness of the techniques which can illuminate internal processing systems. Just as computer programmers need to learn code before they can write programs, it is helpful for you to learn how to distinguish your emotions and thoughts before selecting behavioural patterns. Being aware of what you are thinking and how you are feeling places you in a position where you can choose (and be responsible for) your own actions.

As an English teacher, I believe one of the easiest ways to recognise thoughts and emotions is to be mindful of language techniques such as symbolism, metaphor, connotation and personification. As you develop your understanding of how to recognise and use these techniques you can provide yourself with a means to communicate more effectively (both with yourself and with others). This awareness may enhance your performance both within your *World of Expression* and, in the outer *Library of Life*.

Are you ready to learn more about
how language functions?

These tools can help you
write your

MyStory.

An Introduction to the Conscious and Unconscious Mind

Reflect for a minute on all of the processes that occur within your mind. Think about your actions, emotions and thoughts. What are you aware of doing, and what occurs automatically? Put very simply, your *conscious* is the aspect of yourself that you are actively aware of and your *unconscious* is the aspect of yourself that you are not actively aware of. For example, the unconscious mind directs your brain to process the shape recorded by your eyes so that your conscious mind becomes aware that you see a tree, a flower or a blade of grass.

The unconscious aspect of your mind is responsible for operating, maintaining and preserving your body. It stores and organises your memories, it notices and makes associations and it accommodates emotions. Therefore in very simplistic terms, it is possible to view your unconscious as an administrative hub for managing your actions and reactions. However since the activities of the unconscious mind are less obvious than those of the conscious mind, it is often easy to overlook unconscious programming. Nevertheless, just as a person who has a comprehensive understanding of the back-end functions of a website will be able to create functional, imaginative front-end web pages, so too will an awareness of your unconscious increase your ability to write the pages of your life.

Although it is not my intention to offer a detailed explanation of how the unconscious mind works, I thought I would share a few ideas based on the ideas presented by Bruce Lipton in his book *The Biology of Belief*. Lipton explains that the unconscious mind only processes the present and does not recognise time. So, while the conscious mind may be busy planning the day and reflecting on the future, the unconscious mind manages the behaviours required of a given situation. Lipton suggests that 'the conscious mind offers us free will' but unconscious 'programming takes over the moment your conscious mind is not paying attention.'[7]

Have you ever walked home from school and
suddenly realised
you could not remember the journey?

In this instance your mind was probably on autopilot. It ensured you turned into the right streets while you were thinking about something else.

A second example demonstrates how fears gain form. If a dog bites a young child, their unconscious mind may process the information as 'dogs bite'. As the child grows up they may not consciously remember the initial incident, however their unconscious mind recorded the information and holds it in a form of present stasis (a kind of suspended reality). Often this leads to a fear of all dogs.

Hopefully you are beginning to suspect the extent to which your unconscious programming has an influence on your conscious actions. This relationship between your conscious and unconscious mind can be very powerful. You may like to think of it this way – each second your mind is exposed to data, a veritable cornucopia of sensations, sights, sounds and smells bombard it each second. Your mind must sift through this information and choose what to be consciously aware of. This process occurs in milliseconds, every millisecond.

To illustrate this idea, I would like you to pretend you have decided to buy a red car. Over the next few weeks, each time you go out onto the street, you would most likely notice hundreds of red cars. Does this mean that there are suddenly more red cars on the road? No. It simply means that your conscious mind has

---

[7] Bruce Lipton, *The Biology of Belief,* Hay House, 2010 ed. p.139

focused its attention on red cars. In other words, your unconscious has directed your conscious mind to be more aware of red cars.

The more mindful you are of this connection between your conscious and unconscious mind, the more you can harness it into a cooperative force. This requires recognising your unconscious programming. In a figurative sense, many of these programs may be understood in terms of emotional and thought-based lines of code. Deciphering this code is possible if you GRASP (remember page 21) thoughts and emotions. From here mindfulness or intentional awareness and acceptance of self, is possible. This is important because, as you have been learning, self-awareness tends to increase self-responsibility. In other words, you can begin to understand that the only actions you can control are your own. Equally you may start to appreciate that you choose a response to particular stimuli. In effect you can acknowledge thoughts and allow emotions before choosing to act.

Before taking the next step
along the learning path
take a moment to
listen to your
thoughts and feelings.

Approach

The aim of this exercise is to listen to your thoughts and feelings.

Gather: Sit in a quiet place and close your eyes.

Take five deep breaths.

Each time you exhale, let go of any expectations or frustrations and notice how you relax a little more deeply.

On the sixth breath, ask yourself, 'Who am I?'

Open your eyes to write down your response

_____

Close them again

On the seventh breath, ask yourself, 'Who am I?'

Open your eyes to write down your response

_____

Close them again

On the eighth breath, ask yourself, 'Who am I?'

Open your eyes to write down your response

_____

Close them again

On the ninth breath, ask yourself, 'Who am I?'

Open your eyes to write down your response

_____

Close them again

On the tenth breath, ask yourself, 'Who am I?'

Open your eyes to write down your response

_____

Close them again

Reflect &
Analyse   Look at your responses objectively. What do they
                 suggest about you?

Synthesise: Go for a walk. As you walk listen to a playlist
                 that includes:

                 • One 5 – 10 minute recording that opens your
                   mind to possibilities e.g. a motivational speaker
                   or story about a person who has achieved success
                   in their chosen field.

                 • Two motivational songs. Choose songs which
                   have a positive message in the lyrics and a fast
                   beat. (I listen to songs such as 'Eye of the Tiger'
                   – Survivor and 'Walking on Sunshine' – Katrina
                   and the Waves.)

When the playlist has finished walk in silence for 5 – 10 minutes and pay attention to the thoughts which arise.

Propose: You may like to record your thoughts in a journal when you get home.

Symbolism and Dreams

Thus far your unconscious has been described as a data processing program. Just as a computer program uses a series of 0's and 1's to represent commands, your unconscious mind tends to process information symbolically rather than being bound by time or reality. Information simply is.

In English classes, you were probably told that a symbol represents an abstract thought, feeling or concept. For example, a common symbol for love is ♥. Remember, when considering the meaning implicit in these representations it is important to note the difference between a symbol and a sign. A sign generally has a fixed meaning, such as ♀ for man and ♂ for woman, whereas symbolic meanings tend to be more contextual. For instance, the colour blue may symbolise peacefulness in one situation, relaxation in another and sadness somewhere else.

Symbols can be extremely useful since they expand our understanding of a particular concept. Yet their use extends far beyond this, especially when attempting to gain access to unconscious programming. In fact, it is possible to reflect on the meaning assigned to particular symbols and use this information to gain a greater awareness of thoughts and feelings.

Remember earlier, I used an example of a child being bitten by a dog to illustrate unconscious fears. Imagine this child is now a student in Year 10. They are writing a poem about loyalty and their teacher has asked them to use symbols to represent their feelings. It is highly unlikely that this student would use a dog to illustrate being faithful because, to them, dogs are vicious monsters.

What other symbol might they choose?
Which symbol would you choose?

Just as the above example demonstrates how an interpretation of a symbol offers a window to thoughts, our impression of what a symbol means may also reveal clues about our emotions. For instance, recall what you were thinking when you read that the colour blue may represent peacefulness, relaxation or sadness. Perhaps you related more to one of these explanations than the others. However in a different place, at a different time, your choice may vary. In other words, your choice may reflect your current mood.

In many ways this is like our dreams. In a sense, each aspect of a dream may be seen as a representation of an emotion, thought or idea. Therefore we may view dreams as a series of symbols. In this case our dreams may offer clues about the internal world of expression. However, it is important to realise that dreams are personal. They function as your inspiration since they are part of your imagination.

There are many theories about dreams; why we dream and how dreams may be used. However, it is not my intention to explore the psychology of dreaming here. Remember, I am an English teacher. For me, dreams are like personal stories which may be critically evaluated in a similar manner to analysing a novel or film. In fact, since dreams are often flights of fancy, they represent a wonderful opportunity to explore our imagination using the concept of symbolism. In essence we can see thoughts and emotions represented in a figurative fashion.

Before exploring how to recognise
conscious and unconscious
thoughts and feelings,

would you like to take a short detour
into the land of dreams?

Story: Dream Speak

'What was that?'

A sharp scream sliced the evening air.

Jerked awake, gasping for breath, Liz fought to recall where she was and why she was there. Moving furtively through her thoughts, she fell back against the pillows and warily sought to remember.

Her heart pounded. Her body was blanketed in sweat.

The desire to solve the riddle fought with the panic it inspired. Ever so slowly, as if peeling a bandaid to reveal the wound beneath, Liz pushed to the edge of her consciousness trying to focus on the letters dancing just out of reach. Like demented moths they teased and taunted with their frantic movements.

She closed her eyes and willed herself to concentrate. 'It began with an E, maybe there was an A and a U and perhaps an N ... Enau ... Eaun ...'

The word would not take on recognisable form. And yet ... the feeling it represented was a tangible presence. It was like a malevolent force that sucked the life from its victims.

Shivering, Liz rose cautiously from her bed and moved towards the desk to switch on her computer. The familiar start-up tune chimed its welcome as the light from the screen valiantly repelled the night shadows. In an ironic twist of fate, tonight, the familiar red, blue, green and yellow letters wore a beige and black hounds-tooth check and sported a deer stalker hat.

Liz forced a wry grin. 'Well, Sherlock, nice to know you're here when I need you.'

With growing confidence, she started punching in the letters she had seen. E, U, N, A.

Nothing.

... At least nothing useful.

She kept searching, trying different combinations. Maybe the 'A' was an 'I'?
Anubis –Egyptian god of the afterlife.
Enuki – Powerful Babylonian Earth spirits.

Although either could have represented the force that woke her, Liz wasn't sure. The dream had taken on that fuzzy aspect which comes with wakefulness. She could recall being at home, walking listlessly from room to room. Grey walls hemmed her in, closing around her and then the letters came. She ran. Terrified and helpless, she was desperate to escape their demonic fury.

But they followed.
And followed.
And followed.

Until finally,
she woke up.

Taking a notebook from her desk drawer, Liz returned to bed, snuggled into the covers and began to map out what she remembered. The physical action of writing had an oddly soothing effect. The words were tangible reminders of wakefulness and the letters were locked onto a page. A page in a book that could be closed. She was in control.

She kept writing. The words became sentences, the sentences became paragraphs. While Liz wrote and reflected, a reassuring confidence was kindled inside banishing the lingering feelings of dread. Whatever it was, Liz felt she could fight it. She was aware now, she was ready.

Content, she slept.

* * * * * *

It was an innocent article in a nondescript paper. But ... there it was, a terrier yapping in her ear. A reminder in black and white.

The word!

Ennui.

She googled.

Ennui: *weariness and discontent resulting from satiety or lack of interest; boredom.*

Realisation surged through her and, like an electric current, it infused very pore. This was the malevolent force! A flight of negativity and resentment that had cloaked itself in disinterest and boredom. Disconnected letters that had chased her away from something she loved. Liz decided her dream had been a message; a real wake-up call.

Liz made a decision. She would not become a victim of her own apathy. She was awake, alert and eager to find her own way.

Dream Detour

How often do you dream? Do you remember what you dream? Have you ever said to a friend, 'Guess what I dreamt last night' or 'I had this really weird dream'?

Dreams can be fascinating. It is not uncommon to find a dream intriguing enough to want to share it. However what is perhaps more interesting, are that the stories we create to explain them.

What are dreams? I like to think of dreams as a visual representation of the electrical impulses within my creative centre. They are the symbols created by my unconscious; the language of my imagination. Dreamwork, in this case, involves uncovering this internal language. I find this process offers a window into my own unique system of expression. Interestingly, Stephanie Meyer said she wrote her famous 'Twilight' series based on a dream[8].

The key words to remember are, 'my own unique system'. Although it is possible to buy dream books which claim to translate common symbols, for our purposes they should be avoided. The aim of this detour is to develop a better understanding of your inner world of expression. Therefore, it is important to ask yourself questions and consider what a particular image symbolises to you. Remember, your interpretation of a symbol offers clues about your internal programming. If a friend appears in your dream it is more likely that they represent an aspect of yourself rather than a message about your friend. As you think about what your friend symbolises to you, you can gain a better understanding of yourself. In other words, it is your dream so it represents your ideas about your creative world.

I enjoy the process of dreaming, both the unconscious dreams of my sleep and those dreams (or hopes) I consciously create. In a sense I believe my unconscious dreams provide the inspiration or power to ensure my conscious dreams become reality. They offer

[8] http://www.stepheniemeyer.com/bio.html

a vision of my internal *World of Expression*; a world I can access when I write *MyStory*.

Optional Approach

Write:

Keep a notebook and pen by your bed.

As soon as you wake, record your dream. Write down everything you remember. Record what you recall seeing, hearing and feeling.

Later in the day, consider the symbolic meaning of each aspect of your dream. Ask yourself, what does this image, place, or person mean to me? Remember to consider the personal relevance of each symbol; this is you, communicating with you.

Write down the ideas, explore and reflect on their relevance to aspects of your life. Use what you learn to apply a creative approach to a particular task or idea.

GRASPing your Stage Technique

Earlier you learnt about symbolism and the difference between your conscious and unconscious mind. Perhaps you even took the detour to drift into your dreams and awaken creative imagination. Hopefully your mind is opening to the rich potential that lies within the interdependent relationship between your conscious and unconscious mind. This is the stage for your *World of Expression.*

To boost your performance, you may like to GRASP techniques that can help you learn more about (and therefore gain mastery over) yourself. In other words, it is possible to become more consciously aware of your emotions and thoughts and then to actively use this understanding to achieve your purpose. It simply requires you to consciously:

- Gather internal data – thoughts and feelings.
- Reflect upon those thoughts and feelings.
- Analyse and question how those thoughts and feelings influence your perspective.
- Synthesise thoughts, feelings and perceptions.
- Propose fresh programs.

All successful writers use tools. In fact, at school you have probably spent many English classes identifying language techniques and analysing their effect. And, if you are anything like the students in my classes, you have probably questioned:

- Why do I have to learn this?
- How is this relevant?
- Do you really think the author was thinking about all this stuff while they wrote?

My response to these questions is simple. Yes, the author was consciously thinking about the formation of sentences and how the sentences may be arranged in a meaningful, coherent manner. Yes, the author was purposefully choosing words which would elicit a specific response or evoke a particular emotion. Therefore this is relevant because it offers the opportunity to become aware of subtext or, the meaning within the meaning. Learning about language techniques can increase the effectiveness of your overall communication skills (both with others and yourself) because the knowledge provides evaluation tools.

Therefore, an understanding of how language works places you in a position of power. It helps you gain greater alertness. Think about it this way, being aware of language techniques and their role is like recognising the glue, nails, and screws. It is like knowing about brackets, joints and hinges, or detecting cogs, pistons and pulleys. In other words different language techniques either hold everything in place or they create movement. Therefore, just as a mechanic or electrician uses their knowledge of motors and circuits to evaluate the efficiency or safety of a machine, we use our knowledge of language to evaluate the data presented to us during the communication process.

Of course the important word here is 'evaluate'. At the heart of GRASP is the skill of evaluation. Recognising the function of language techniques will help you evaluate the data that is presented to you, both by others and yourself. In other words when you understand the role of language techniques, you will have a measuring tool to determine how accurate, helpful, valid or reliable information is. Then you can make a conscious decision about how, or even if, you want to use that data.

Remember, as you have learnt in the earlier sections of this scaffold, you choose your own actions and the only person's actions you can direct are your own. Nevertheless, as human beings we are social creatures who live in community groups. Therefore we usually search for feelings of connection and association. It is for this reason that communication is so important.

However, gaining mastery over language techniques delivers so much more than effective communication skills. It offers the opportunity for effective inner dialogue. In other words, awareness of how language functions can alert you to patterns in your self-talk and therefore, may provide deeper insight into your emotions and thoughts. In other words, language techniques have the potential to provide a method of evaluating your inner world so that you may function more effectively within your outer world. Essentially this is what I am referring to when I speak of boosting your performance by 'GRASPing Stage Techniques'.

So, what are the main *Stage Techniques*? Your English teacher has probably encouraged you to use language techniques such as similes, metaphors, personification, repetition and rhetorical questions. You may also remember teachers mentioning analogy, symbol, connotation, juxtaposition, irony, alliteration, assonance and onomatopoeia. The aim here is not to review language techniques, rather I would like to focus on how you can use some of these techniques outside the classroom and within your *World of Expression*. You have already seen how you can use symbolism to enrich your appreciation of your imaginative world, now we will consider metaphors, personification and connotation.

Are you ready to *GRASP*
staging techniques?

Will you allow your emotions
and
acknowledge your thoughts?

Step 5 on the *Learning Path*

Allow your emotions.
Be emotionally aware

Step 1 encouraged you to peer inside yourself and discover who you are.

Step 2 asked you to 4C your future.

Step 3 proposed the discovery of your own place.

Step 4 offered the opportunity to uncover your Honour Compass.

Now it is time for the fifth step.

How do you feel?

Step 5: Allow Your Emotions

How frequently do you notice the range of emotions you feel within a month or even a week? Are you aware of the different emotions you feel within a single day? Some of these emotions may be enjoyable, while others may not. Russ Harris, in his book *The Happiness Trap*[9] reminds readers that there will be times when we are not happy. He also cautions that intense emotions may be difficult to control.

However, even if it may not be easy to command feelings, in most cases, it may be possible to recognise an emotion, determine if it is helpful or unhelpful (in a particular situation), appropriate or not appropriate (at a given time) and then, allow it or let it go.

In other words, it may be possible to acknowledge the emotion and observe the accompanying thoughts before choosing how to respond. In this instance we can take whatever learning is needed and watch the rest pass. In fact, as Harris points out, it is usually the resistance to a particular emotion that creates a sense of pain. Resistance (and the frustration caused by a perceived inability to control a situation) frequently results in elevated feelings of anxiety. Really what I am suggesting here is that even though the emotion can be difficult to choose, it may be possible to choose a behavioural response to that emotion that will make the emotion easier to manage. Nevertheless, the ability to make this choice requires discipline, responsibility and commitment. As has been repeated throughout *MyStory*, you have the power to choose the place of the author, rather than that of the character.

Since becoming the author is easier when you have a greater understanding of yourself, it is important to become more consciously aware of how your emotions affect your thoughts and how your thoughts influence your emotions. In a sense, your

---

[9] Russ Harris, *The Happiness Trap*, Exisle Publishing, Australia, 2007

thoughts and emotions are linked in a symbiotic relationship where one feeds the other and vice versa. Sometimes it may seem as though the emotion rises first, triggering a thought that escalates that emotion, which then enlarges the thought until the emotion explodes. However, other times the thought may be recognised first. Either way, the chain reaction is usually the same. Perhaps at this point the expression, 'being blown out of proportion' may make some sense. Imagine how much more in control (and more confident and compassionate) you could feel, if you had a diffusion strategy.

In the movie Never Back Down Jake's coach cautions him:

No matter what happens, control the outcome.

Essentially, in this scene coach Roqua is reminding Jake to be aware of his emotions and channel them towards his desired outcome, rather than letting emotions override his values. He is reminding Jake that he has a choice.

Remember, in the previous chapter, you learnt that we each have the power to choose and that generally, our choices are a response to a perceived need (such as respect, acceptance and love). Marketing professionals often use this idea to encourage consumers to buy a particular product or service. They highlight a pain motivator to direct consumers toward a particular behavioural response. However, if you recognise your emotions and their effect on your actions, it is possible to identify marketing hype. This greater awareness places you in a position of control since you are better equipped to make a choice based on your values, rather than your emotions.

Think about this, the author of a story selects the characters and then develops their personality and strengths. The author decides where the character will go and places challenges along their way. The author determines if, and how, the character will overcome

149

these obstacles. The author chooses which thoughts and feelings the character will experience. Of course as the author of your *MyStory*, it may not be possible to pluck an emotion from your imagination, however it is possible to identify the emotion and use it in such a way as to develop your *MyStory* rather than experiencing an emotional hijack.

Three techniques which can help you become more consciously aware of your emotions are: metaphor, personification and connotation. I will show you how mastery of these techniques can improve not only your communication skills, but also your ability to communicate with yourself.

However, let us first look at two different emotion / thought chains.

- I *feel* lonely → I think, I have nothing to do → I *feel* sad → I think, my friends are ignoring me → I *feel* neglected → I think, my friends are not my real friends → I *feel* angry.

  or

- I *feel* lonely → I think, I would like to see my friends → I *feel* hopeful → I think, we could go to the beach → I *feel* excited → I think, I will call my friends → I *feel* happy.

Of course this is a very simplistic example and our emotion and thoughts are usually intertwined rather than following a simple linear pattern. Nevertheless, it is possible to recognise the relationship between emotions, thoughts and actions. If we recognise a chain in process, we have a greater chance of directing the flow.

I have used the phrase 'directing the flow' deliberately; this metaphor has a particular connotation. Reflect for a moment. What image and feeling does the phrase evoke? Does it influence your interpretation of what you have read?

Hopefully the phrase 'directing the flow' encouraged you to recall the times you have heard emotions referred to in liquid forms; have you heard the expression 'a sea of emotion'? This is important. If we think of emotions as tides ebbing and flowing we can imagine them as a fluid force and allow them to flow over and around us, rather than attempting to bottle them up. To illustrate this concept, I will use metaphors.

Metaphor

Remember what you have learnt about similes and metaphors at school. A *simile* is a comparison using 'like' or 'as'. For example, 'she is <u>as</u> cold as ice'. A *metaphor* is a comparison where one object, idea or feeling is called the other – 'she <u>is</u> ice'. One of its main functions of similes and metaphors is to make a concept more tangible. Writers and speakers use them to create a vivid or coherent image which enriches the communication process. These techniques are particularly relevant when exploring the complexity of emotions. In other words, since they can make a concept clearer, they make it easier to transmit an idea from one mind to another.

So why use a metaphor rather than a simile? Let's consider the 'she is as cold as ice' / 'she is ice' examples. As you read these two comparisons what impression do your receive? In most cases the metaphor connotes a stronger or more powerful feeling through the direct image created. After all, if she is described as ice and we picture a block of ice rather than her, she has become almost dehumanised. She is now something cold, desolate and other.

This 'dehumanising' aspect of metaphors can be useful because it offers the opportunity to evaluate an idea, concept or action from a detached third party perspective. In this instance we can be objective rather than subjective. This is why metaphors can be helpful when exploring the impact of emotions. Think about it this way – sometimes it is easier to recognise an emotion if we give it tangible form. Using metaphors, it is possible to take an emotion outside of our body, recognise it as a sensation and see that emotion for what it is. This is often the first step toward choosing what we want to do rather than taking commands from our emotions.

Since metaphors create meaning by offering a picture of one thing in the place of another, they have been used throughout *MyStory* to illuminate complex or abstract ideas. Hopefully, as I use metaphors to help you learn, you will recognise how to use the technique yourself. In other words, you can develop the ability to use metaphors to clarify your thoughts and feelings which you may then share with others, in a meaningful way.

The three metaphors which follow aim to illustrate the concept of *allowing emotions*. As you read, think about how these extended metaphors enhance your understanding of a concept. You may also like to use these metaphors as a model to formulate your own metaphor to explain your reaction to an emotional situation.

First, imagine swimming at the beach. You may like to see yourself enveloped in clear, blue water. You will notice the soft golden sand which graces the shoreline and feel the bubbling white foam as the gently breaking waves dance across your skin. The sound of laughter fills your mind and you feel simultaneously relaxed and invigorated. Then, all of a sudden, you sense an unpleasant pull away from the shore and the once friendly waves seem to rise malevolently, threatening to draw you down into a swirling abyss.

You have been caught in a rip.

What would you do?
How would you feel?

Would you blame the ocean, cursing and screaming for it to let it you go? Would you believe the ocean hated you and had been silently waiting for an opportunity to destroy you? Would you feel guilty for taking the time to swim or disappointed that you chose to swim today? Would you feel frustrated with yourself for not recognising the danger?

Of course, you are likely to feel a degree of fear.

But, how will you respond?

Life guards suggest allowing the tide to carry you further out to sea. They warn that if you resist the straining tide and attempt to swim against it, you will soon tire. If you continue to resist, you may find yourself sinking beneath the battering waves. However, if you were to use your energy to stay afloat, swimming parallel to the shore and simply let the water carry you, you will soon find yourself riding out the rip and eventually be free of it. While it is true you are likely to be a considerable distance from where you started (or where you wanted to be), you are likely to find yourself better equipped (not as exhausted), to swim back to shore.

Of course to truly survive in this metaphor, you need faith in your capacity to swim. That is to say, you need faith in yourself and your abilities. With self-confidence and a sense of balance, you would feel buoyant and aware, realising that once you had ridden out the rip, you could swim back to shore. Yes, you are likely to feel tired, but you will return to firm ground.

This is why I believe it is so important to learn how to swim – and here, even though I am speaking in both a literal and a figurative sense, I will concentrate on the figurative meaning. In other words it is important for you to develop your emotional strength and sense of balance so that you may ride out the challenges, obstacles and barriers which arise. Realistically speaking, life is not a flat line and in all honesty would you want it to be? (Remember a flat line on a heart monitor indicates an absence of life.)

Elizabeth Gilbert in her book, *Eat Pray Love*[10] offered another useful metaphor. She likened her mind to a harbour which gave

[10] Elizabeth Gilbert, *Eat Pray Love*, Bloomsbury Publishing, London 2007ed. p.188

access to the island of herself. Using this analogy she suggested that it is possible to choose who (which thoughts and emotions) we allow to berth in our harbour. In other words, after we have noticed and recognised an emotion (or thought), we can choose whether to allow it right of entry or to watch while it sails past.

Another rather gross metaphor which I have used when talking to students who were anxious about an examination result, involves a figurative scab on your arm. Chances are, if you repetitively picked away at it, continually exposing the wound underneath, it would leave a scar. However, if you acknowledged the pain and decided to focus on what you could do in the future, rather than this current hurt, the wound would eventually heal. The important message here is to focus on what you *can do* (such as use the examination result as a diagnostic tool for identifying the skills you need to develop for the next exam) rather than what you *cannot do* (travel through time to change the result). In directing your attention to what you can control, you are placing yourself in the author's space and from here, internal confidence and courage can inspire the creative energy required to discover a fresh approach to future challenges.

Nevertheless, it must be acknowledged that there are likely to be times when your internal resources are depleted. To return to our rip metaphor, even the strongest of swimmers may find themselves fatigued or out of their depth. In these instances they rely on their support network; friends, family, coaches, trainers, mentors and teachers who offer assistance, guidance and encouragement. Other times they may even require a lifeguard, a professional who is trained to save lives. In these cases, the swimmer raises their hand and the lifeguard swims out to give aid.

Similarly, there are likely to be times when challenges or emotional upheavals seem overwhelming. At these times, rather than resisting, a better alternative is to raise your hand and ask for help. This is the courageous alternative. In deciding to ask for help you are acknowledging your situation, you are taking a proactive approach and making the choice to manage your situation. In this case you can remain the author of your *MyStory*.

Identify the emotion.
Determine if it is helpful to the situation
and then,

let it in
or
let it go.

Connotation

Are you beginning to perceive the power of metaphors? Hopefully you can see how using them may help you clarify your feelings and enrich the inner and outer communication process?

Now we are going to go a little deeper into the *World of Expression* to focus on the words themselves. Words are powerful. They have the ability to encourage and to destroy. Marketers use words to elicit specific behaviours – so do bullies. However, coaches and captains use words to inspire.

The movie *Remember the Titans* provides numerous motivational speeches. If you watch the film you will see a training session where Coach Boone leads the team to the Battle of Gettysburg site. While there he reached out to the boys, explaining:

> *'This green field right here, painted red, bubblin' with the blood of young boys ...You listen, and you take a lesson from the dead. If we don't come together right now on this hallowed ground, we too will be destroyed.'*

Similarly, in the film *We Are Marshall*, coach Lengyel stood at the gravesite of six Thundering Herd team members who were killed in a plane crash. Like Boone, Lengyel used setting and words to reach into the emotions of the team:

> *'They don't know your heart. I do... When you take that field today, you've got to lay that heart on the line, men. From the soles of your feet, with every ounce of blood you've got in your body.'*

In each of these examples, specific words and phrases were used to elicit an emotional response from the characters (and the audience). It is interesting that both coaches refer to 'blood'. Blood is usually perceived as a life force, an essential commodity

157

within the body that feeds internal organs. By evoking the image of blood, coaches Boone and Langyel are appealing to an essential energy core within their players, and this engages emotions. The coaches (and scriptwriters) understood that when a person's emotions are involved, they are more motivated and thus more formidable. Put simply, when a person's emotions are engaged they are capable of enormous things.

The power of this emotional energy is clearly evident in the film *X-Men: First Class*. If you watch this movie you will find out that learning how to harness and focus emotions is the key skill Charles (Professor X) wants Erik (Magneto) to master.

The extent to which a word evokes a particular emotional response generally rests within its connotation. In your English classes you may have learnt that 'connotation' refers to the emotion attached to a word or, as one of my Year 8 students liked to say, the word's *vibe*. As a technique it is used by writers to prompt a specific emotional response within the reader. Advertisers use this technique frequently to persuade consumers to purchase. For instance, you are more likely to buy a figure-<u>hugging</u> dress than a figure-<u>squashing</u> dress.

However, critical readers recognise these emotional associations and evaluate how they influence our understanding of what is being said. Why is this important? To answer this question let me ask you another. Which synonym would you substitute for the word 'negative' in the sentence below?

> *Recognise negative emotions and what inspired them and then, gently and deliberately, detach from them.*

Words such as unhappy, pessimistic, depressing, harmful and unhelpful could work equally well in this sentence. However, each word has a slightly different meaning and connotation.

Chapter 3: The Stage

How will you determine which meaning is most applicable?

Usually you would look at the context of the word within the sentence and then substitute the word which appears most relevant. However your guess will be limited by your understanding of the context. Your understanding of the context will be influenced by your perspective, and your perspective is likely to be influenced by your current emotional state. This emotional state is likely to be influenced by your perception of how well your needs are being met. For instance, have you ever noticed how you seem to feel happier when you feel refreshed and more confident when you feel happy? Conversely, if you are feeling tired you may become easily frustrated and believe a task is beyond your capabilities.

As you are probably realising, every time we read, we are making assumptions about the intended meaning. In many cases, we are also assuming that others are making the same assumptions, and ... have you heard the old saying about the word 'assume' – it makes an 'ass' out of 'u' and 'me'?

Therefore, two people can read the same sentence and interpret it in different ways. Similarly we may say one thing but the person we are communicating with hears something else. This is a source of many misunderstandings. In some cases, we may even mind-read, and I am not talking about paranormal activity. Rather I am referring to the times we imagine we know what someone else is feeling. For instance, a friend may say,

I need to stop.

You may feel frustrated and think your friend is tired or lazy, but maybe they simply want to tie their shoelace.

My aim here is to encourage you to see how emotions, and even the emotional attachment we attribute to words, may influence our interpretation of a situation. This interpretation usually influences our behaviour and the emotional pull may be significant, especially if we feel as though something we value is being threatened. This shows the importance of understanding the link between values, emotions and thoughts. Coaches are able to harness the will to win (or not lose) by reminding players to tap into their own internal strengths and inner pride. Coaches encourage players to seek glory and to move toward their intended purpose by deliberately choosing words which reach into players emotional reserves.

However, in some cases, a fear of losing something valuable may have a weakening effect. This usually occurs when we feel as though we do not have access to renewable inner resources. At these times, the more we perceive something as valuable, the more we fear losing it. Often these fears result from a belief that there is not enough and we expect to miss out. We forget the strengths inside us and succumb to inhibitive and limiting belief systems which leave us reacting to a situation, rather than choosing a response.

Hopefully you are beginning to see how all of this is linked to your understanding of yourself and the strength of your 4Cs. The more confident, courageous, creative and compassionate you feel, the more likely you are to perceive abundant supplies of whatever it is you need, and the less likely you are to fear losing it. In other words, when these resources are within, you have an awareness that you hold the power to generate what you truly need. Therefore you will be more likely to flow toward something you aspire to, rather than avoiding something because you are afraid of it.

Therefore, to return to the earlier message of allowing our emotions, instead of resisting them, it is important to recognise your feelings, learn what is useful and then let them go. From here you can focus on what you actually value and actively move toward what you need, rather than running away from what you do not. In other words, you may begin to focus on what you can do, what you have control over, rather than feeling as though you are a victim under the thrall of someone else.

Personification

Are you beginning to appreciate the depth of thought and language awareness that the author dedicates to the communication process? Words are chosen deliberately and images are crafted with precision. One more technique which you will find helpful is 'personification'.

Like metaphors and connotation, personification aims to provide clarity and emotional appeal. Just as metaphors create meaning by offering a picture of one thing in the place of another, personification builds awareness by attributing human characteristics to something which is not human. For instance 'the tree reached toward the sky'. In this example, the reaching tree offers the impression of a tree with a particular purpose. Since the process of reaching is a recognisable human behaviour, the audience is encouraged to personally relate to the action of the tree. In a sense, personification focuses attention on the relationship between the audience and writer, and may be used to explore cause and effect associations. This is particularly useful when considering emotions. Put simply, sometimes, imagining emotions as a person or a physical entity makes them easier to distinguish; the emotion becomes more recognisable or more familiar and thus, easier to relate to.

Elizabeth Gilbert frequently personifies emotions in *Eat Pray Love*. For example, while in Italy, she describes loneliness as a 'goon' who 'barged into her life'.[11] This offers the reader a clearer vision of both Gilbert's emotional state and the impact of emotions such as loneliness.

Similarly, although not personification in a strictly literal sense, a number of books, films and television programs demonise emotions in order to focus attention on their debilitating qualities. For instance, *Buffy the Vampire Slayer* and *Charmed* frequently

[11] Elizabeth Gilbert, *Eat Pray Love*, Bloomsbury Publishing, London 2007ed. p.55

employ demonisation techniques to draw emotions such as fear, greed or anger from the body and then place them in a physical demonised form which could be physically fought and slain. A specific example is found in *Fear Itself*, an episode from season four. Throughout this episode, Buffy and her friends are forced to confront the external manifestations of their fears, some of which take human form. At the conclusion of the episode, viewers learn (as the characters do) that we often personify fear or imagine it to be a much bigger creature than it actually is.

In fact, viewed at a figurative level, programs like *Buffy* can be a fascinating foray into the challenges faced by young people. Creators such as Jos Weldon use the fantasy genre to explore fears, vices, motivations and triumphs. They combine the techniques of symbolism, metaphor, personification and connotation to represent concepts within humanity. They create, within the cinematic arena, a world which may be shared and analysed by viewers.

As the author, you have a similar power. You may reach into your *World of Expression* to GRASP your *Staging Techniques* and write your *MyStory*; a story which nestles cohesively within *The Library of Life*.

Reflect

1. How do you respond when a situation does not seem to work out the way you intended?

2. Can you accept there will be times when you will be confronted by challenges, hurdles and barriers?

3. Do you understand that there will be times when you feel unhappy or lonely or annoyed?

4. Imagine a situation which has evoked a strong emotional response in the past. Think about how you responded at the time.

5. Recall the emotions you were feeling. Use personification to describe them.

6. Can you think of a metaphor that would illustrate these emotions?

Approach

Create   Develop your metaphor from the previous approach question into a short story. Use personification at least once to describe an emotion. Think carefully about the connotation of the words you use. Include this short story in your *MyStory* journal or blog. You may even like to share your story by submitting it to www.isthismystory.com

Story: Finding Gold

The balmy summer evening wrapped itself around the wide pedestrian strip as the animated chatter of tourists mingled with a local busker belting out tunes for a tolerant audience. Sam didn't notice. It was a night alive with expectation, enthusiasm and excitement; a paradise which promised adventure, but all Sam could see was trouble. He ignored the neon lights which danced their way across the pavement, instead he was wary - intent on keeping a discreet distance between himself and his family. There were people everywhere and the last thing he wanted was for someone to think he was here with his oldies. Sam was sure that someone in this motley crew of extended family was going to do something embarrassing – someone like Nana Rose.

Nana Rose was watching the crowd. In sudden excitement she hollered, 'Wait … I need to get a picture of Bill with one of the Meter Maids. This is the first time he has seen them.'

Her animated tone whipped through Sam's fragile sense of space. He melted into the pavement. He felt like the roles of the Wicked Witch and Dorothy had been reversed. The Wicked Witch lived while he … he had become a shimmering puddle on the footpath. He wished he could seep through the cracks in the pavement. Like Dorothy, he wanted to be home, he wanted to be somewhere over a fricking rainbow, elsewhere, anywhere, as long as it was far away from the humiliating antics of his impetuous grandmother.

How could she do something so … so … so dumb?

Shooting an exasperated glance at her reticent grandson, Rose hailed the passing bronzed beauties. Two girls, dressed in sparkling gold bikinis and draped with golden sashes, stopped and smiled.

Sam tried to merge with the crowd who had stopped to watch. He wanted to escape, but his father's voice carried.

Chapter 3: The Stage

'Wait ...' his father, Rob, called out.

Rather than risk drawing attention, Sam sunk in on himself and adopted what he hoped was an indifferent pose.

Sidling over to Sam, Rob explained, 'You know Sammy boy, the Meter Maids are something of a Surfers Paradise icon. Although technically they were employed by the council to feed coins into expired parking meters, their main aim was to promote the town. So, when the meters were removed, the Meter Maids stayed. Today they attract publicity and share a friendly smile with the thousands of people who visit each year.'

Sam scowled and looked at the ground. His dad sounded like someone who had swallowed a tourist brochure. Anyway, he didn't care. He just wanted to be out of there. He didn't want anyone to notice what his grandmother was doing.

Why didn't she understand? You're not supposed to go up and talk to them, you had to wait. Wait until they talked to you. And no way would they let you have your photo taken with them. What was she thinking? They were going to say no, and Nan would feel ...

What! No way!

Sam watched in disbelief as his predictions collapsed in disarray. There was Granddad standing, proud and tall between two of the most gorgeous girls Sam had ever seen. Nana Rose merrily clicked away, ignoring the crowd gathering to watch. Sam shook his head, amazed at his grandmother's boldness.

How did she do it? What was her secret?

Ever since Sam could remember, Nana Rose did things her way. She didn't dress like a grandma, she didn't talk like a grandma, and she certainly didn't act like a grandma. When he was younger Sam loved this about her. As he got older, he hated it. Nana Rose just didn't care what others might think and Sam found that embarrassing. Yet tonight, Sam's stomach churned as he watched in bewildered silence. He began to question those feelings. Nana Rose seized every opportunity to make life memorable, while he … he was still waiting for something awesome to happen.

'You should go over and get one too. Go on, I know you want to.' Rob smiled conspiratorially.

With a nonchalant shrug of his shoulders Sam replied, 'Yeah, maybe.'

Inside he was a swirl of emotion. *Maybe he could get a photo. Maybe it was okay. Maybe people wouldn't laugh. Maybe the girls wouldn't say no.*

Maybe …

Unfortunately the effort to appear indifferent came at a cost. Time had passed and the opportunity to capitalise on the groundwork laid down by his indomitable grandmother slipped away. The girls had moved on.

'That's okay. Just go after them,' his mother, Tina, urged.

'Naw … doesn't matter.' Sam tried to sound bored, but one glance at his mother's perceptive expression warned him he had not been successful. He slouched off, taking the lead toward their chosen restaurant before anyone could question him further.

Inwardly Sam fumed. He kicked himself and berated his lack of courage. He railed against the injustice of his world; a space where fear held him rigidly within a tight circle of feigned indifference. At 14 he was a shifting mass of confusion and bravado with an identity that oscillated between hoping for attentive admiration and wanting to remain unnoticed in the shadows.

Once seated for dinner the Fyrth family engaged in a lively exchange of holiday reminiscences replete with hyperbole and punctuated with exclamations of how quickly the holiday had passed and how they couldn't believe they were returning home tomorrow. Sam sat quietly behind a wall of self-recrimination. Eventually, unable to contain the emotions that battered his brain he finally spoke.

'What am I doing? I should have just asked, why didn't I?'

Nana Rose looked at Sam. 'What did you think would happen?'

'Ah, duh … Like she would have said no!'Sam let the sarcasm drip unchecked.

'So, what of it? You would still be sitting here, in exactly the same position, enjoying dinner with us. Probably photoless. But … you wouldn't be angry at yourself. And you wouldn't be playing the endless *what if* game.'

Sam searched his grandmother's wise eyes. Fathomless pools of gentle kindness, they offered respite from the swiftly changing tides of his self-confidence. He made a decision.

'You're right. You *are* right. I'm going to do it.' Excitement resonated in his voice. 'When we walk out of here, I'm going to find those girls and I'm going to ask them to have a photo taken with me … and if they say no …well … who cares!'

Once he was outside the security of the restaurant Sam's fears resurfaced. It was one thing to make an announcement to his family within the sheltering confines of the restaurant, but quite another standing out on the busy street scanning the bustling crowd for a glimmer of gold. Still, he was determined. Sam believed this was one of those defining Hollywood moments where the hero must choose between walking into the cave or skulking in the shadows.

Threats of the unknown always seemed to inspire the greatest fear. Sam hated not knowing the outcome. He detested not being able to predict the result. But ... he reasoned, maybe, to some extent, he could. The girls could say yes, or they could say no. Either way he would know that he had taken action over the variables he could control.

169

He re-examined his options. The known feelings of regret over a wasted opportunity were weighed up against the unknown promise of taking a risk. Then he realised success was simply a matter of perspective and how he chose to view the situation.

'There. They're over there.' His sister pointed.

Sam's heart began to pound. With a mouth like parchment and body that felt on fire, the Olympian sprinted.

'Wait, Sam,' his mum called after him. 'You forgot the camera.' Turning to Rob she quickly added, 'I'll follow him and we'll meet you back at the hotel.'

By the time Tina caught up with Sam, he was deep in conversation. A wide smile graced a glowing face and his eyes shone with happy strength.

'Oh yeah, here's Mum with the camera.' Sam stood with the confidence of a champion between two glamorous girls.

'Thanks heaps.' Sam smiled and waved as he rejoined his mum.

'I did it, I really did it!' Conviction danced inside him, cartwheels of success rolled through every nerve fibre. 'This feels amazing … I feel like I could do anything!'

Step 6 on the *Learning Path*

Manage your emotions.
Monitor how you *really* feel

<u>*Step 1*</u> *encouraged you to peer inside yourself and discover who you are.*

<u>*Step 2*</u> *asked you to 4C your future.*

<u>*Step 3*</u> *proposed the discovery of your own place.*

<u>*Step 4*</u> *offered the opportunity to uncover your* Honour Compass.

<u>*Step 5*</u> *invited you to recognise your emotions.*

Now it is time for the sixth step.

Are you ready to process what you're feeling?

Step 6: Manage Your Emotions

Your recent steps along the *Learning Path* have brought you to this stage, the figurative meeting point between your conscious and unconscious mind. In order to boost your performance, you have learnt how to use the techniques of symbolism, metaphor, connotation and personification to GRASP your emotions and develop mastery over the art of communication. Understanding how to use these techniques as evaluation tools can help you recognise internal dialogue and reframe a situation. You can choose to view an emotion and the thoughts attached to them from a different perspective and then either act on them or allow them to drift past.

Can you imagine a way to use these techniques to monitor your emotional approach to some less than pleasant emotions?

Fear

Fear is one of the most debilitating of emotions. It rises from inner depths to form pools of self-doubt, frustration and resentment. It may trigger jealousy, greed and anger and often leads to worry, anxiety and depression. Common fears include:

- not being good enough
- not being skilled enough
- not being capable enough
- not being strong enough
- not being smart enough
- losing something we love
- losing someone we love

In many instances, fear becomes a constricting force that binds and restricts our actions. As a result we may refuse to participate in an activity or we might deliberately supply a poor effort (thus providing ourself with an excuse for failure). Often these choices, born of fear, grow into negative consequences.

However what is it we are really frightened of? Is it:

- rejection
- ridicule or
- disappointing those we care about (and who care for us)?

Have you ever asked yourself how real your fears are – have you questioned if they could actually develop into a physical reality?

*Often fears are simply **F**alse **E**vidence **A**ppearing **R**eal.*

Of course it should be noted that fear is a natural response and, in many cases, a necessary one. Our bodies seem to be hardwired to respond with the flight-or-fight response. This is a survival mechanism. However, it is equally important to recognise the programs soft wired into our brain and distinguish how real a fear is. Often a fear is simply a mental construct, rather than being a genuine life-threatening situation. In fact, fear is usually in the future. We imagine possible outcomes by playing the 'what if' game till it becomes an endless loop of disaster scenarios.

Did you watch the Buffy episode, *Fear Itself?* If you did, you would have seen how fear can take control. Body, mind and spirit descends into a maelstrom, a whirling vortex, which threatens to consume giving rise to desperate, reactive responses. However, as was the case in this episode, often a fear is much larger in the mind than it ever was in reality.

The key is to distinguish between genuine threatening situations and the ones that are of the mind. Then you can take steps to control the aspects that are within your sphere of influence.

Is This *MyStory*

Look at your fears.
What is it you are really afraid of?

How real is it?

In many instances, the belief system which feeds a particular anxiety, upon closer inspection, takes the form of an expectation. In these cases, it is this belief that you are expected to do, be, act or behave in a particular way that leads you to question your ability to perform. This questioning fertilises doubt and then that doubt gives birth to fear.

I have seen students fall into this abyss. I have fallen into this void myself – most of us have. In almost all cases the culprit was an unsubstantiated belief that I had to do something, be someone or achieve something, coupled with doubt that I could do, be or achieve.

If we accept this reasoning, conquering fear becomes a process of looking 'through' anxiety to the expectation which is giving it life. Often these expectations are of our own creation. Since we have created them, we have the ability to deconstruct them. We can use techniques such as metaphor, personification (remember the Buffy episode) and connotation to examine our self-talk and uncover emotional programming. In effect, pulling emotions out and deconstructing them it is much the same as pulling the sheet off a piece of furniture to discover a simple utilitarian object is not the 'ghost' we perceived it to be. In these situations we can reframe our perspective and choose an appropriate behaviour.

Reflect

1) What do you fear? Look carefully at each of the fears listed below. Decide if any of the fears apply to you and then ask yourself:

   i) What is the worst thing that could happen?

   ii) How likely is it to happen?

   iii) What aspects can you control?

□ Losing friendship

i)

ii)

iii)

□ Losing the respect of your peers

i)

ii)

iii)

□ Not passing a test, exam or assessment

i)

ii)

iii)

What did you notice as you completed this reflect section? How did you feel as you were responding? Did you recall earlier steps along the *Learning Path*; steps which encouraged you to use your

Honour Compass and generate internal power using confidence, courage, creativity and compassion?

Remember, the *Learning Path* is your rite, with each step you are developing the skills and techniques that will help you write your story. These inner tools cannot be lost because they are part of you. Your stage is within your place. This is your *World of Expression* and you have the management role.

You can choose to open your eyes.
You can choose to close them.
You can choose your focus.

Your emotions
follow that focus and
your actions follow the emotion.

Failure

Fear holds hands with its mate 'failure', so it is worth spending some time examining your perception of it. Unfortunately social attitudes towards failure are frequently negative. Arguably, this perception arises from a competition-fuelled belief that divides people into winners and losers. Some believe if they do not win, they have wasted time and energy. In other words, they do not recognise the skills they gained while in the pursuit of victory, unless they win.

This obsession with winning heightens stress and encourages 'away' behaviours (a reactive response to escape or move away from a perceived threat) rather than 'towards' behaviours (a proactive approach that involves active steps toward a desired outcome). Competition can also lower feelings of self-worth, especially when a person compares their achievements to the achievements of others. Similarly, if attention is focused solely on an outcome, the magic (or lifelong learning) within the journey may be overlooked. However, competition can become a motivating force especially if you take the time to 4C your future. This requires you to move beyond reactive programming and focus on what has been achieved.

Incidentally, the idea that the journey is as important as the final destination was beautifully explored in Paulo Coelho's allegorical novel, *The Alchemist*. At a surface level, this story describes a shepherd boy's quest for treasure. However, metaphorically, the book presents an illuminating illustration for living a purposeful life that recognises the gift in the present. Stories such as *The Alchemist* demonstrate how adversity may provide the opportunity to learn. In these cases, winning becomes a simple matter of perspective. In other words, if the primary goal is to learn, grow or improve skills, it is not necessary to win first place in order to triumph. A person who recognises the value in the journey 'wins' because they improve their skills, knowledge and experience. Of course, a person needs to accept the learning in order to realise this positive outcome. Although, winning in this instance is not the same as coming first, hopefully you can see that you do not have to 'come first', in order to achieve.

One fortunate consequence of valuing the journey is adopting a different approach to failure. In essence, what I am suggesting is that it is possible to reframe your view of failure so that you recognise it as a signal which directs you along a new path to fresh opportunities, rather than perceiving it as a threat binding you in self-doubt.

To illustrate this point, I usually ask students to think about the reasons for having a blood test. This analogy is particularly useful for those who worry about upcoming exams, or who are disappointed by examination results.

When a doctor examines the blood, they are not looking for a winner or the person with the best blood, rather they are seeking a match or a diagnosis. From one point of view, it may be possible to fail a blood test; your blood may not be compatible, or it may contain evidence of something that should not be there i.e. a virus. However, rather than judging you for being unsuited or berating you for being sick, the doctor will use the knowledge gained from the test to find a suitable match or to suggest a course of action that can improve your health. Therefore the failure can be reframed and the belief re-adjusted to reflect a result, rather than a negative comment about capabilities.

We can view tests and exams at school in much the same manner. Examinations are designed to position students within a class where their needs will be best met or to test what they know; and that is all they are designed to do. In other words examinations are a diagnostic tool. They are simply a way of gauging what learning had the most relevance and what a student could devote more attention to in order to improve their proficiency level. They are not, nor will they ever be, a measure of self-worth.

It has been my observation that people who consider tests to be a measure of self-worth are frequently locked in a vicious competitive circle that, if examined closely, probably reflects their attitudes towards themself more than anything else. In this case, a fear of failure may be a signal that a person has yet to find their inner anchorage point; their stage of internal balance. Can you recall what you read about fear? When you face your fear of failure you are likely to realise that the perceived threat is much smaller than you imagined.

Remember, as you have learnt, when you discover your place of inner strength the renewable power generated by confidence, courage, creativity and compassion can help you to reframe your view of failure. In this case, failure may become a precision tool which directs your focus toward skills and understandings yet to be learnt.

At this point I would like to offer a brief note to anyone studying for an important examination (such as a university entrance exam) who may be thinking,

but this examination will determine my future.

If you find yourself in this position I would like to suggest you look closely at the chattering monkeys of your self-talk. Here, I am using the popular phrase 'chattering monkeys' to depict those hyperactive and oft time overly animated thoughts that tend to assume a life of their own. These creatures exaggerate a situation, worrying away at it as they leap from one extreme to the next. However, it is possible to arrest their flight. Take a few deep breaths and then ask yourself,

will the test determine my future,

or

will my actions determine my future?

In essence, my challenge to you is to take responsibility for the variables that you have control over and focus on them, rather than the threats (real and imagined) you do not have control over. In other words, actually do your best rather than trying to do your best (remember Yoda's advice to Luke). So:

- Make a study plan, and follow it.
- Ask for assistance from teachers.
- Seek support from family and trustworthy friends.
- Establish a study group.
- Develop relaxation techniques.

And, most importantly,
accept responsibility for your actions.

Accepting Responsibility

Once again I would like you to recall the earlier pages which examined the emotion of fear. Fear often arises from an expectation, a feeling of not having enough, or not having sufficient control over resources or a situation. However, if we focus on what we actually have and the choices we can make, we may take the lead in our own life. In other words, when we accept responsibility for our choices, we move out of a fearful position and into a position of courage.

This idea of accepting personal responsibility was demonstrated in the move *Take the Lead*. Based on the true story of Pierre Dulaine, the film shows how learning to ballroom dance may teach an individual teamwork, dignity and respect. My favourite scene is when Dulaine, explained to his students,

The man proposes the step
and it is the women's choice to accept.

Here, simply put, is a message about choice and control. We can choose to cooperate or we can choose to fight against a mistaken belief that someone else is trying to dictate our actions. Understanding this concept is one of the most important steps in moving from a victim mentality to position of strength.

This idea of self-responsibility is also explored, in the novel *To Kill a Mockingbird*, Atticus explained to Jem,

I wanted you to see what real courage is, instead of getting the idea that courage is a man with a gun in his hand. It's when you know you're licked before you begin but you begin anyway and you see it through no matter what. You rarely win, but sometimes you do.[12]

---

[12] Harper Lee, *To Kill a Mockingbird*, Arrow Books, London, 1997ed, p.124

Here Atticus was referring to Mrs Dubose's decision to take responsibility for her life, rather than remaining a victim to her addiction to morphine.

We can use these examples as illustrations. They show how overcoming fear, particularly a fear of failure, is possible when we reframe or re-adjust our perspective and recognise that we have more control over a situation than we initially thought. However, accepting this responsibility usually requires us to acknowledge our feelings as our own, rather than them being someone else's fault.

Perhaps an example will help make this clearer. Think for a moment, does this phrase sound familiar?

'X' makes me unhappy because they are mean to me.

This statement suggests that you have given the responsibility for your feelings to someone else and, to a large extent, it implies you have given someone else authority over you. But you can regain control by accepting responsibility for your feelings. This is where courage replaces fear. When you accept responsibility for your feelings you are in a position of control. Imagine how much more assertive and confident you would feel if you said,

'X' behaved in a manner I am not willing to accept.'

Can you hear the difference? In this statement you have indicated that you understand you have a choice to accept, or not accept, the behaviour.

Can you see how being responsible for your actions and identifying how you feel about the actions of others allows you the freedom to choose a response? When you accept responsibility for yourself – for your emotions and actions – you place yourself in a position to write your story. This places you on a stage where you direct your own life rather than following a crowd. When you own your emotions you are less likely to feel threatened by the opinion of others.

Reflect

The example below is a model and as such may not faithfully replicate real life. My aim is not to offer an infallible solution, rather I hope to encourage you to recognise the link between emotions, thoughts and actions.

Of course, there will be times when an emotion rises so quickly it is difficult to manage. Nevertheless, even if the emotion bursts forth with geyser-like intensity, you can recognise that it is your emotion and as such, you can chose to learn from the experience. Talk about the experience with a mentor or experienced counsellor – they can help you perceive the situation from a different perspective and offer strategies that can help you respond differently in the future.

Remember, this scaffold is simply a map. It is a tool which you can choose to use to discover more about yourself and your actions.

Recall a situation where you blamed someone else for your feelings.
My brother makes me feel so frustrated when he comes into my room.

Phrase the situation taking ownership of your emotion.
I feel frustrated when my brother comes into my room.

Look at the thought underneath the feeling of frustration.
I think my brother does not respect my privacy.

Look at the situation from a different perspective.
Maybe my brother wanted to spend time with me, or my brother needs my help.

Manage your feelings in terms of the new perspective and think about which actions you can control.

I <u>feel</u> compassion and <u>ask</u> my brother exactly what it is that he wants (rather than yelling at him to get out of my room) and <u>negotiate</u> a solution where I can <u>offer</u> help and he can remember to knock before he comes into my room.

1. Follow the model above and think about how you could take ownership of your emotions in two hypothetical situations.

   i) My teacher makes me feel angry.

   ii) My friend makes me feel unhappy.

Approach

Write: Write a blog post or journal entry that explores your reactions in the past and how you could react differently in the future by focusing on the actions you can control, rather than the actions of someone else.

Perception

Have you ever stopped to examine the feelings that arise when someone does not share your opinion?

- Perhaps you thought you were being personally attacked.
- Maybe you felt betrayed.
- Perhaps you thought your ideas were not valued.
- Maybe you felt angry and frustrated.
- Maybe you reacted aggressively to protect your ideas.

Could you have responded in a more constructive way? In other words, could the situation be reframed or seen from a different perspective? Could you have chosen to view the disagreement as an opportunity to see an alternate point of view? Is it possible to see a difference in perspective, rather than an idea that is better or worse than the one you proposed?

In *To Kill a Mocking Bird* Atticus advises Scout:

> *You never really understand a person until you consider things from his point of view ... until you climb into his skin and walk around in it.*[13]

Put simply, it is useful to remember that two people may view the same data but perceive different outcomes. Earlier we referred to a similar theory when we discussed the different programs used by computers – have you ever tried to open a document, written on a PC, with a Mac computer? Unless the file had been saved in a shared file format, all you are likely to see is a series of strange symbols.

One analogy I like to use in the classroom is:

---

[13] Harper Lee, *To Kill a Mockingbird*, Arrow Books, London, 1997ed, p.11

Chapter 3: The Stage

Even though we may sit in the same room,
we sit on our own chair.

What does this actually mean? It means that even though we may live in the same city, attend the same school and be in similar classes, we experience events and view situations through individual sets of eyes.

With this in mind, it is worth noting that our attitudes towards others are often influenced by the closeness of their values to our own. This is largely because they reaffirm our perspective or point of view. They are sitting next to us, which usually means they see a similar view, hear similar sounds and feel similar sensations. As a result, we are more likely to feel comfortable with the people who sit next to us since they share our perspective and their affirmation seems to prove that our point of view is correct. Since their ideas validate our own, our sense of belonging is reinforced and we tend to feel more secure.

But what if people do not share our opinion; what if we sit in isolation? Or, what happens if the people we care about sit on the other side of the room? Parents, siblings and friends may not always share our point of view and we may feel bereft and unsupported.

However we can learn to accept alternative perspectives. This is because we have the capacity to choose how we feel about the attitudes and behaviours of others. We can choose to feel negatively toward a particular behaviour, or we can choose to feel positive. We may even choose to feel indifferent.

The key factor in our ability to manage emotional responses is our ability to be self-aware and feel self-confident. If we are self-aware and self-accepting, we do not require external affirmations and may sit in the same room, in our own seat, harmoniously, respectfully and contentedly while still acknowledging other people's right to sit in their own chair.

Reflect

1. How do you feel toward a person who disagrees with you?

2. Why do you feel this way? Is it possible to feel a different way?

3. Can you think of a situation when you misjudged a person or situation? How did you behave? How would you like to have behaved?

Perception and Projection

As you are realising, many of your behaviours are a response to a feeling. These feelings are generally linked to a thought. Thus far, we have discussed the value of recognising these emotions and allowing the feelings that arise, so that you can choose a response rather than resisting and reacting. Hopefully, you have also begun to appreciate the benefits to be found in managing your emotions and accepting responsibility for your own actions.

Sometimes the traits we like least within others are the characteristics we do not like to admit in ourself. Fear of acknowledging these traits may leads us to project those qualities on to others because it is easier to fight someone else than acknowledge our own less desirable traits. However, this inner doubt can sabotage our relationships. You may recall we briefly touched on this idea of projection when we discussed using your *Honour Compass* to choose behavioural responses which harmonise rather than destabilise.

This is why I have continually suggested that a more constructive approach is to take responsibility for your emotions and make a choice rather than blaming someone else for your actions. One of the best illustrations of this concept that I have seen can be found in the Star Wars movie *The Empire Strikes Back*. Earlier I referred you to the scene where Yoda reminds Luke:

'Do ... or do not. There is no try.'

In a later scene, as Luke approaches the final phase of his training Yoda instructs him to enter a cave. Metaphorically this represents a process where Luke is to look within himself and face his inner fears. As Luke walks with tentative determination through the cave, he encounters an illusion of his enemy, Lord Vader. The two battle and Luke beheads Vader. However, to his shocked dismay, Luke discovers the face behind the dark mask is actually his own. We may use this scene as a reminder that sometimes, the dark forces which we attribute to an alien or outside force, may actually be an inner fear.

However, it is possible to reach inside to your *World of Expression,*

Uncover your Honour Compass.
Locate your 4C generator.
Accept responsibility for your action,

and

conquer fear.

Conquer Fear through Self-Confidence, Flexibility and Knowing How to Learn.

Confidence provides the power to overcome fear and being confident is a choice. It is choosing to be alert to the aspects of your life that you can control and making the decision to step purposefully along the *Learning Path* towards your destination. These steps are made easier by a flexible mindset which acknowledges different perspectives.

At the beginning of *MyStory* I suggested that the ability to learn places a master key in your hand. Think of it this way – flexibility of thought, when combined with the secure belief that you have the ability to learn, provides the confidence of knowing you have the internal skills required to meet any challenge.

In a sense, flexibility acts as a lubricant which eases your way along the *Learning Path*. Flexibility is a skill you can develop. Athletes and dancers improve their physical flexibility through repetitive practice which trains their muscles. In much the same way it is possible to train your mind. Coaching your mind requires the commitment to GRASP your life. Using the learning strategy of GRASP builds mental flexibility because it requires you to gather information, then reflect and analyse it so you can synthesise the data into new combinations which propose a fresh approach. The repetitive application of this process trains your mind to be flexible by alerting your consciousness to novel solutions rather than being locked in a rigid past.

This is why you attend school, to develop the mental strategies that train your mind to solve problems. Remember, it is the skills, learnt at school which are important. These physical processes are usually more significant than the content itself. Content is easily accessed through modern technology, and it changes rapidly. This is why flexibility and an understanding of the processes involved in learning are so important. Combined, they can provide the confidence to appreciate and embrace the change that is so prevalent in a rapid-paced world.

The value of developing a flexible mindset is simply illustrated in a short metaphorical book by Dr Spencer Johnson entitled *Who Moved My Cheese?*[14] Contained within its pages is a short story about two mice and two mice-sized men who are forced to cope with a changed access to resources (cheese). The mice pragmatically and determinedly adapt to their altered circumstances and go in search of new supplies. Similarly, one of the men recognises and confronts his fears. He develops a new flexibility which yields positive results. The other man keeps returning to the same empty room, each time with the same expectation, and each time he discovers nothing. The metaphorical message is clear – success is much easier to achieve with a willingness to adapt.

It has been said that Einstein defined 'stupid' as repeating the same action over and over in the expectation of a different result. How often have you found yourself repeating past actions in the hope that this time it will be different? Do you hand in essays following the same structure, expecting a better mark, only to find you have again received a fraction of what you thought the essay was worth? Why? Could it be that a fear of attempting something new binds you to familiar patterns?

Often, a belief that change will restrict access to resources, or an unfamiliar situation will require skills yet to be gained, promotes puddles of fear. Experiencing security within a wave of change may seem like a paradox, yet it is more likely to be achieved if a person has confidence in their ability to GRASP new information. Why? Because being confident in your ability to consider evidence and propose your own ideas develops flexibility. It creates a mindset that reminds you that you are capable of managing your thoughts and actions. Importantly, it provides choices and offers evidence which supports making that choice. You can experience a sense of

---

[14] Dr Spencer Johnson, *Who Moved My Cheese*, Vermilion, London, 1999.

self-assuredness because you understand that even if you do not know something, you have the skills to learn it. It is these tangible reasonings that provide handholds of security. You are less likely to fear change or an unfamiliar situation because you have faith in your ability to adapt.

Remember fear is the enemy of achievement; it is the demon that thwarts the desire to move forward into unknown territories. However, with a flexible mindset, confident attitude and a willingness to GRASP life, you can have the tools to achieve whatever it is you set out to achieve.

The next step on your *Learning Path* will help you acknowledge your thoughts and identify limiting beliefs, because achievement of purpose also requires determination.

Are you ready to GRASP new ideas
and develop
flexible thought patterns?

<u>Step 7 on the *Learning Path*</u>

Acknowledge your thoughts.
Be thoughtfully present

<u>*Step 1*</u> *encouraged you to peer inside yourself and discover who you are.*

<u>*Step 2*</u> *asked you to 4C your future.*

<u>*Step 3*</u> *proposed the discovery of your own place.*

<u>*Step 4*</u> *offered the opportunity to uncover your* Honour Compass.

<u>*Step 5*</u> *invited you to recognise your emotions.*

<u>*Step 6*</u> *called upon you to process your feelings.*

Now it is time for the seventh step.

What do you think?

Step 7: Acknowledge Your Thoughts

At this moment, how comfortable are you upon your stage?

- Do you stand at the centre, aware of the techniques that can illuminate your internal processing systems?
- How mindfully do you attend to your emotions?
- Are you alert to your self-talk?

As you have learnt, gaining mastery over techniques such as symbolism, metaphor, personification and connotation can help you communicate with yourself. They are tools which can assist in the management of emotions. Similarly, these techniques may help you monitor and master your self-talk so that you can direct your inner dialogue with care and precision. In essence, acknowledging your thoughts can help you restrain the chattering monkeys. Therefore, choosing to be aware of language patterns offers the opportunity to:

refer to what you want,
rather than what you don't want.

Purposeful Self-Talk

Earlier in the chapter I introduced you to the concept of a conscious and unconscious mind. Remember, in every second the mind is being bombarded with data. It collects this data through the five senses (taste, touch, sight, hearing, smell) and files the information as thoughts and feelings. Since it is impossible to be actively aware of every piece of information, a filtration system is applied to determine which pieces of data have most relevance to a given situation. This explains why we suddenly notice more red cars on the road after we have made a decision to buy a red car. Put simply, information we need now is positioned in the conscious part of our mind, and data we may need later is stored in the unconscious. Interestingly, and worth noting, is that sometimes the information filed away may become distorted. If you have ever sent a text message that was embarrassingly altered by prescriptive text you will know what I mean.

Consider these two sentences:

- I must remember to feed the dog.
- I must not forget to feed the dog.

Now look carefully at each sentence. Perhaps you will notice that even though the meaning of both sentences is the same, in the first sentence you are likely to focus on *must remember* whereas, in the second sentence, your attention may be drawn to *must forget*. In this example, the smaller word not is easily over-read or ignored. If your goal is to ensure the dog is fed, which sentence is likely to ensure your objective is met?

Remember language is a powerful tool. It offers a system for transferring information and, when used deliberately, can direct the thoughts and emotions which influence our actions – remember connotation; are you more likely to buy a figure-hugging dress or a figure-squashing dress? This is why choosing to be mindful of self-talk can be extremely powerful, especially in terms of your self-esteem.

Motivational strategies such as repeating positive affirmations and posting inspirational messages on walls relies on the theory that words influence actions. Of course, the more internally synced these words are, the closer they align to your value system, the more authority they carry. If your self-talk is a reflection of how you view yourself, and you are in the author's position, obviously it is important to give yourself the words that focus on

what you want to achieve.

This is why affirmations really only become useful when they are internally inspired.

This idea of 'say it the way you want it' and figuratively planting ideas within our unconscious was explored by Napoleon Hill in his book, *Think and Grow Rich*[15]. Although first published in 1937, this book has been reprinted hundreds of times and many of the ideas contained within it make for interesting reading. Of course, as is the case with any information, it is more useful to GRASP the content and apply what has relevance to you in terms of your values rather than accepting the ideas as truth. Nevertheless, I would like to share with you some of Hill's ideas about a concept he called 'auto-suggestion'.

Hill suggests that we can *plant* a specific
idea, strategy or thought
into our unconscious and, if we nourish that
idea, strategy or thought,
it is more likely to become a tangible, physical manifestation.

[15] Napoleon Hill, *Think and Grow Rich*, www.ThinkAndGrowRichGifts.com.au

This works on the principle that our focus will be directed towards the

idea, strategy or thought,

so we become attentive to the

idea, strategy or thought

and recognise opportunities that arise in relation to the

idea, strategy or thought.

This awareness can become a *purposeful behavioural pattern.*

This practice of auto-suggestion is based on the premise that the unconscious mind does not distinguish between what has actually happened and what is imagined to have happened, nor does it process negatives. Auto-suggestion also stands on the belief that the unconscious mind relies on repetition to install a habit.

A simple way to see auto-suggestion in action is to consider your reaction to the phrase:

Don't look down.

In most cases, you will instinctively look down because your unconscious mind has focused on the command look down and not recognised the negative, *don't*. Therefore a better instruction would be:

Look towards the destination.

Hill also suggests that any idea planted in the unconscious has the potential to grow and, just as the earth does not distinguish between a weed or a flower, your mind has the capacity to support both helpful and unhelpful thoughts. Following this gardening metaphor, the more attention you give to your thoughts, the more they are likely to grow. Therefore, if your self-talk focuses on what you do not want, you may find that is exactly what you get.

For example, compare the self-talk:

I have no money.

to

I want to earn more money.

In the first example, you may be tempted to wait, worry or complain about your financial circumstances. However in the second example, you are more likely to focus on identifying strategies which can improve your financial circumstances. In the first example you *sit*, in the second example you *do*.

Similarly, can you see how telling yourself,

I am useless at studying.

can be rephrased as

I do not have the answer yet.

Hopefully you are beginning to realise that saying what you want rather than what you don't want can direct your attention toward purposeful action. Purposeful action is more likely to yield the desired result than waiting for some mystical external happening. The true magic is internal; you need to take action to achieve your purpose. You need to actively move toward your destination.

If you sit and wait
for someone else to perform an action
so you can get where you want,
you may wait for a long time,

but

if you take action,
you are in control,

so

make a commitment
take the steps toward your destination.

Chapter 3: The Stage

Perhaps at this point I should point out that saying it the way you want it is not the same as positive thinking. In fact, I would like to suggest that positive thinking or

wishing for something hard enough and
saying it aloud often enough and
writing it down frequently enough,
will not guarantee you achieve
what you want to achieve.

Achievement requires action. It takes dedicated effort. You have to actually do, more than you say. While it is helpful to have an optimistic attitude and to have faith in your abilities, these feelings are only powerful if they are authentic. In other words, they should come from within and be synced and balanced.

Saying the way you want it is simply a map for your unconscious mind. Remember a map is only a directional tool, it is not a magic carpet.

You are the author.
Acknowledge your thoughts
and
take action
to reach your chosen destination.

Move from a Character Mentality to an Author Mentality

Making the transition from a character in someone else's story to the author of your own requires commitment. Remember, the act of writing is a physical one. In other words, it is your responsibility to turn your emotions and thoughts into tangible realities. However to stage a success story, you also need to move beyond limiting belief systems. Again, this requires a conscious decision to move with determination along the *Learning Path* toward your destination.

Flexibility of thought, an enthusiasm toward learning and a willingness to see beyond what we thought to be true may help uncover the opinions underpinning a belief. This process can offer freedom from restrictive programming.

In Bram Stocker's *Dracula*[16], Professor Van Helsing wanted Dr Seward to open his mind to the possibility that Lucy had changed into a vampire so he asked Dr Seward to:

> *believe in things that you cannot ...*

He reminded Dr Seward that faith

> *... enables us to believe things which we know to be untrue.*

Seward replied,

> *Then you want me not to let some previous conviction injure the receptivity of my mind with regard to some strange matter.*

Dr Seward needed to change his perspective in order to take the steps necessary to defeat Count Dracula. Stoker used the characters

---

[16] Bram Stoker, *Dracula*, Penguin Classics 2003 ed, p. 206

of Van Helsing and Seward to encourage readers to keep an open mind, particularly when faced with potentially troubling thoughts. In other words, when we are willing to view a situation from a different perspective, we are more likely to uncover a solution rather than waiting and wishing things were different. Put simply, new thoughts can provide new solutions.

Therefore, the transition from the restrictive belief programs of a character, to the constructive mindset of the author may be made easier by reflecting upon the validity of the thoughts underneath a particular belief. With a flexible attitude, it may be possible to choose new thoughts which are more pertinent to a particular situation.

A person with a character attitude habitually believes they lack the resources, skills, or ability to control a situation. This often leads to feelings of fear, resentment and even jealousy. However, if the thoughts behind these emotions are examined, they can usually be reframed. This process of changing perspective and consciously redirecting self-talk can build an author mindset which supports achievement, rather than propping up evasive, excuse-laden inaction.

Moving from a character attitude to an author mindset requires more than flexible thinking, it requires action. The author has a victorious attitude and takes responsibility for their actions in order to achieve success and reach the desired destination. A character plays the role of victim and blames everyone else for their situation. A character *waits* for someone to hand them something whereas the author *makes* things happen.

It is possible to move from the characters role to the position of author, the choice is yours.

1. Recognise that a belief such as 'I'm not good enough' or 'It's too hard' is probably an excuse that is inhibiting your ability to achieve. In most cases, this excuse is linked to a fear. Use

metaphor or personification to explore your feelings and identify what you are nervous about. If you can isolate the fear, you may provide yourself with an opportunity to see it and confront it.

2. Determine which resources you have control over and focus on what you can do, rather than all of the reasons why you can't do something. Centre your attention on the areas within your sphere of influence rather than those on the outside. Make a conscious decision to do what you can do.

3. Remember, the only person's actions and emotions you can control are your own, so take ownership of your thoughts and emotions.

4. Take responsibility for the actions and outcomes you can influence (rather than assigning blame to someone else for how you feel). Accept the consequences of your actions.

5. Learn from mistakes – view a negative experience as an opportunity to learn.

Chapter 3: The Stage

Move from a belief
that binds you to a character's role
to a mindset
which promotes you to author status.

Reflect

Think of an occasion where your beliefs restricted your actions, e.g. *I am not good at Maths*. Ask yourself,

1. How do I know ....I am not good at maths?

2. What would happen if I didn't think ....I am not good at maths?

3. What specifically does ....not being good at maths mean to me?

4. If I thought ....I was good at maths what could I do?

Approach

Write: Use your responses to write a blog post or journal entry that explores how you could:

i) make better use of the resources you have control over

ii) focus on specific actions within your sphere of influence

and move towards achieving something you previously thought was too difficult.

LEAF through Life's Pages

Throughout this chapter you have been learning real life applications for the techniques used by writers to craft a story. In particular, we focused on symbols, metaphors, connotation and personification as language techniques which broaden a reader's understanding. These techniques enable critical reflection by alerting audiences to the conceptual ideas within the subtext. However, as you have seen you can also use these techniques to read your thoughts and emotions. In other words, symbols, metaphors, connotation and personification can help you become more aware of yourself and your relationships with others. These techniques provide tools to monitor and manage your self-talk.

Before moving on to the final chapter of *MyStory*, there is one more technique to discuss.

Acronym

Do you remember what an acronym is?
Do you know why they are used?

An acronym is a word formed by the initials of other words. For instance I have used an acronym when I suggested GRASPing your life. Similarly, 4Cing your future may be described as a punned acronym. I have used this technique purposefully because, as single words, GRASP and 4C provide a reminder of their component words. Acronyms can be useful because they shorten complex concepts into a single word thus making the concept easier to remember (this is a great strategy to use when preparing for exams).

Put simply, the word 'grasp', means to seize hold of or comprehend, so when you GRASP your life, you take control of the action of living and gain a greater understanding of your life. This is achieved by becoming more aware of yourself and the world around you. The learning strategy which can help is, gather, reflect, analyse, synthesise and propose. Throughout this chapter, you have been encouraged to GRASP your emotions and thoughts. This action places you in a position to manage your responses by allowing your emotions and acknowledging your thoughts.

In much the same way, when reading 'The Door' chapter you learnt why it is useful to 4C your future. This punned acronym encouraged you to foresee or look forward to your future. It reminded you that the inspirational power to achieve the future of your choice lies within the active development of confidence, courage, creativity and compassion.

Now I would like to propose a third acronym – LEAF. The word 'leaf' refers to the foliage on a tree or, more relevantly in this context, turning the pages of a book. Have you heard the expression *take a leaf from my book?* It suggests following my example. Similarly, *to turn over a new leaf* implies taking fresh approach. Keeping this in mind, are you willing to LEAF through life's pages; as you turn the page, act with **l**ove and **e**nthusiasm, choose to be **a**ware and **f**lexible.

Act with
Love and
Enthusiasm,

by choosing to be
Aware and
Flexible

Story: The Rite III

The path ahead was blanketed in autumn leaves, their rustic tones forming an intricate ecological tapestry. Tania paused to consider her options.

Which way?

She had been travelling for over a month and loneliness sat like a bird on her shoulder. She was tired, footsore and disappointed. Gazing at the path that stretched like an endless line through tall unyielding trees, she wondered why she had ever felt she had the ability to see this through.

Dejected she allowed her legs to crumple.

And she sat.

Just sat ...

And waited.

Overhead birds called and the pungent fragrance of rich earth and fallen leaves mingled with the scent of oncoming rain. A storm was brewing, but there was no-one to notice. Or care.

Tania sat.

She sat for a long time.

And when the rain fell, she continued ...

To sit.

Did this happen to the others? she thought wearily. Day in and day out I walked. I trod the path. I followed the course. I have been optimistic. I have focused on the future. I have carried my tools. I have used my strengths and remembered my training. I have done everything I was supposed to do. But I am still alone and I am still not There. I don't even know where There is. All I remember is that this is the Warrior's Rite.

The rain fell. Bleak rivulets trickled down Tania's dark hair. Insidiously it reached into the folds of her cloak searching in vain for an opening, but the well-cured hide protected Tania from the storm's deepest onslaught. Inside she remained warm and dry.

Finally, the rain simply
stopped.

A steamy warmth emanated from the ground as a cricket's song built a melody to complement frog's croaky beat.

At some point she must have fallen asleep. She awoke to find herself cocooned within the exposed roots of an immense, wizened tree. Tania rose and shook the remaining water from her hair, offering simple gratitude to this ancient guardian.

The forest looked clean. Like a dirty child who had been dragged protesting into the shower, it had emerged from the deluge fresh and apologetic. Somehow it didn't seem so endless. Gathering the knapsack, spear and bow she had carelessly tossed aside, Tania looked ahead to the path.

With straightened spine and raised chin, she began to walk. The lonely bird was still hovering but she focused on the gleeful call of two parrots who surfed the wind's currents. The bright red and green of their plumage seemed to coax her forwards while at the same time, reminding her to remain vigilant. With careful determination, mindful of the slippery surface, Tania trod the path, testing each step before placing her foot firmly on the ground. Her progress was slow and before long her knapsack assumed the same heavy weight of the day before.

Nothing has changed, Tania thought dejectedly. Still she continued, placing one moccasined foot in front of the other.

Do I need to change course?
Where?

Chapter 3: The Stage

The path stretches one way.
Am I supposed to just follow this track forever?
Is this the way?

Tania paused, standing steady in the middle of the track.

Maybe I could …

As she gazed upwards a fresh idea danced into view. With deft movements Tania unslung her knapsack dispatching the lonely bird with a flurry of activity. Careful to place her bow and spear in a safe position, she reached up and grasped a low-hanging branch. Nimble as a cat, Tania climbed from branch to branch, until she felt she was high enough. Then, content with her new vantage point, she looked out across the forest. From this new perspective she could see what had been hidden.

There!

The cave was close, but it lay in the centre, rather than at some distant final point. Excited awareness crackled along her spine pulsing energy into every vital organ.

She was so close.
So close.

Before returning to the path, Tania calculated the distance and looked for the target landmarks that would provide directional cues.

Reminding herself to breathe, she scarpered down the tree to gather her knapsack, spear and bow. Walking in a slow arc, she took note of the view beneath the tree and looked for her positioning cues. Her internal compass thrummed reassuringly while she determined the safest route. With clear eyes Tania glimpsed a slight shimmer. It ran along a faint path that she hadn't noticed before. Turning to this inner track, she set off on the new route towards the centre.

It was *There*.

How do you feel at this moment?
What are you thinking?

Have you noticed
how your thoughts
and emotions
influence your action?

How wide is your perspective?

Where do you stand?
Are you at Centre Stage?

Are you ready
for an audience?

Remember to take a mindful breath.

Chapter 4

The AUDIENCE

Focused Expression

Living and Breathing *MyStory*

Live and Breathe Your MyStory

As you balance yourself upon your stage collecting your thoughts and allowing your emotions, gaze toward the audience.

Who and what do you see?

Often when an author crafts their story, they have a particular audience in mind. Your English teacher would have been referring to this concept when they reminded you to be mindful of 'register'. In other words, appreciating meaning within a particular text is easier if you understand the delicate interplay between audience, context and purpose. In most cases, the writer is consciously aware of the message they want to convey. They direct that message toward a specific audience and deliberately use the features of their chosen genre to ensure ideas are conveyed in a coherent manner.

As you compose your MyStory you may question:

- Who is my audience?
- What is my purpose?
- Where is my context?

You may like to imagine your context being life itself and to live life you need to breathe. Being mindful of your breathing can help you become focused and purposeful.

You may like to perceive your purpose as being a series of progressive targets that direct your progress along the *Learning Path*, as well as being the destination towards which you are moving. Remember your life's story will be more meaningful to you, if you direct it with purposeful intent.

You may like to recognise your audience as being yourself. In essence you are both the author and the person the story is being built for.

Chapter 4: The Audience

This is your life and you have the choice to be responsible for it and to it.

In the previous two chapters you were encouraged to explore the territories inside you and to take the author's place on a centred stage. From this position you may begin to monitor and direct your thoughts and emotions. This final chapter offers strategies for establishing direction, setting targets and determining destination. It will also propose a purposeful mindset that involves breathing and living mindfully.

<u>Step 8 on the *Learning Path*</u>

Define your direction.
Set your target.

<u>Step 1</u> encouraged you to peer inside yourself and discover who you are.

<u>Step 2</u> asked you to 4C your future.

<u>Step 3</u> proposed the discovery of your own place.

<u>Step 4</u> offered the opportunity to uncover your Honour Compass.

<u>Step 5</u> invited you to recognise your emotions.

<u>Step 6</u> called upon you to process your feelings.

<u>Step 7</u> asked you to reflect upon your thoughts.

Now it is time for the eighth step.

Where are You heading?

Step 8: Define Your Direction

As you read *MyStory* you have been moving along the *Learning Path*. From the first chapter you have been introduced to the idea of moving toward a destination and the subsequent pages have brought you to this point. Hopefully you have begun to recognise and appreciate who you are.

Where will you go from here?

Where do you want to go from here?

This is an active decision. It is your choice. Your responsibility is to physically involve yourself in the process of defining your direction and setting targets which will lead you toward a destination.

Remember, the destination is not fixed – life is not a flat line and you have free will. Therefore you are likely to modify your course as circumstances change and your values develop. This is a positive response. It reflects your capacity to learn. When change comes (and it will come), you are more likely to feel confident when you know where you are going. Similarly, you are more likely to feel courageous when you have the skills required or when you,

know that you can learn them.

This is why I have continually emphasised the importance of learning how to learn. My aim is to teach you the steps, so that you have the capacity to GRASP life and make your own informed decisions.

Remember, successful authors write with purpose. They have a message to share; they have a reason for developing the narrative, a reason which is revealed as the story unfolds. Authors maintain audience interest by foreshadowing events that alert the reader of what is to come. In a sense, adopting the targeting strategies which follow may act as foreshadowed messages to yourself. They aim to focus your attention on a desired outcome so that you can move forward with purposeful intent.

In addition to providing directional cues, setting a series of progressive targets can be very motivating. In essence, each target may become a rung on the ladder to successfully reaching a grander objective. Think of it this way, writing a 1000-word essay may sound daunting, but writing five 200-word paragraphs may seem less so, especially when you write each paragraph mindfully. In other words, if you establish a direction for your essay (a thesis or main argument) and have clear target points (topic sentences) you can build each individual paragraph toward a final conclusion. As each paragraph is written you are likely to feel a sense of relief. Before you know it, you will have five carefully constructed paragraphs. Of course you will need to draft and edit your writing to ensure it flows cohesively from one point to the next. However, since the words are written, you will have something tangible upon which to focus.

Are you ready to set your targets?

Would you like to commit to a purpose?

Establishing targets and determining purpose often requires facing fear and recognising procrastination. However, it is also important to allow yourself the freedom to dream.

Are you able to suspend disbelief?

Can you open your mind and let your imagination loose?

Before we continue, a word of advice: a purpose and the targets which lead to it are more tangible if they are in print. Writing them down crystallises intent; and here I am talking about the physical process of writing. I know that typing them into a computer may be faster, but faster isn't always better. Often, because writing is a slower process, your mind has time to reflect. So, even if you enter them into your computer, tablet or smart phone later, write them down first. Writing gives your ideas, feelings and aspirations time to form; conscious dreams become targets; actively focused upon targets become direction and your dreams are more able to assume a reality.

You may like to write targets on sticky notes. These small sticky pieces of paper are easily moved around to organise and sequence target rungs. These rungs can become a ladder that reaches toward a greater purpose.

A Targeted Purpose

Achieving targets requires conscious action. First, you should determine values and vision and check that they are in sync. Then develop your target vision and balance it with your thoughts and feelings. Next build, prioritise and commit to a course of action. Finally, execute the plan and move toward your destination to achieve your purpose.

Write a target.

Plan the steps to achieve it.

Commit to action.

SMART Targeting

A target should be SMART, it should be:

- **S**pecific – say it the way you want it.
- **M**easurable – recognise what it will look, sound and feel like when you have attained it.
- **A**ttainable – know that you can achieve it.
- **R**elevant – ensure it aligns with your core values.
- **T**ime bound – commit to achieving it within a specified time frame.

For example

> *By xx/xx/xxxx I will have my own blog. Each week I use my blog to voice my thoughts and feelings. I feel a sense of achievement and confidence, knowing that with each post, the accuracy and fluency of my writing improves. I post each Sunday night. Each post is a minimum of 250 words. My posts reflect my mood, my experiences and chart my perception of current affairs.*

As illustrated by the above example, it is also useful to write it in the positive and in present tense. In other words, say it the way you want it. Remember, you need to write your target. Writing it down means that you are actively committing to it. Look at it morning and night. Each time you do, imagine the excitement you will feel knowing that you have attained your objective.

Now ask yourself,

What am I willing to do to achieve my target?

Reaching a Synced Target

The likelihood of reaching a target is enhanced when it is authentic. This is why we have focused on learning about you. The more comfortable you become within your skin, the better your position to recognise your strengths and core values, and the more empowered you are likely to feel.

However, be patient with yourself, your inner world is likely to change, just as your outer appearance does. Remember it is possible to grow and develop in a flexible response to environmental changes. This rite is a process; your story unfolds as you LEAF through the pages. So GRASP the techniques which can help you adapt and learn. 4C your future, uncover your core values and use your *Honour Compass* to synchronise your direction.

In an effort to keep it simple, you may like to imagine your targets acting as grid references to the areas you are moving toward. In this case their function is similar to a succession of lighthouses. They offer a course through wild oceans and unfamiliar terrain. However, these lighthouses need to be built on solid ground, rather than on a shifting sandbank of empty promises.

So be honest with yourself and reflect upon your current situation. What do you need to do to make a dream, a target? Are you willing take action and move towards it? What do you need to do to make your target a reality?

Importantly, is this what you truly want?

Does it align with your core values?

Reflect

1. Look ahead to where you would like to be and then list the steps which will take you there.

Currently I am at 'a' _____

I will be at 'b' _____

I value 'c' & 'd' _____

_____

The steps I need to _____

take to move _____

from 'a' to 'b' are _____

_____

_____

Targets with Foundations

As already stated, the more deeply embedded your target is, the more internally generated and inwardly aligned it is, the stronger its foundation and brighter it glows, the greater the likelihood that you will reach your destination.

Would you like to learn some practical strategies

which can help you establish targets?

You may like to try each strategy to determine which is most appropriate for you. You will probably find that some strategies work better for personal targets while others are best suited for academic or extracurricular ones. The main message here is to use strategies which fit comfortably within you.

1. *Write* your SMART target

   Record your target on a card or sticky note and place it near your mirror, bed, in a school folder, in your smart phone or near your computer screen. In other words, place it in a location which has relevance for the target. Look at it morning and night. Each time you do, pretend you have achieved your target and feel the excitement that comes from knowing you have reached your destination.

2. *Harmonise* your SMART target

   Choose a motivational song and change the lyrics to match your target. When you're in the shower, out walking or simply in a place you enjoy being, sing your target song. I find this strategy particularly effective at those times when I feel my passion waning or energy levels dipping.

3. *Visualise* your SMART target

Imagine what it will be like achieving your target. (What does it feel like, what does it look like and what does it sound like?) Build a vivid picture in your mind; give it form and structure. Then feel it, listen to it, touch it, smell it and look at it from every angle. Put yourself in the picture. Remember to place the picture in the present.

4. *Breathe* your SMART target

Choose a quiet place and think about your target. Reflect upon each step between where you are now and where you would like to be. Breathe deeply with each rung on the target ladder. With each breath, notice how you feel as you get closer to achieving your goal. Build within yourself the feelings of confidence, courage and vitality.

5. *Live* your SMART target

Actively place yourself in a position to achieve a dream target. Spend time with people who have already achieved a similar target. This may be real or imagined (i.e. you can read books and watch films about people who have achieved success).

Similarly, if there is a relationship you want, become the person who has that relationship. In other words, treat others the way you would like to be treated.

Reflect

Use the questions below to develop a targeted approach to improve your results in a particular subject.

1. Where are you now?

   i) Which skills and content do you feel most comfortable with?

2. Where do you want to be?

   i) Which skills would you like to develop this term?

   ii) What content would you like to understand?

   iii) What mark (or improvement percentage) would you like to achieve on the end of year exam?

3. What will you do to get there?

   i) What specific strategies will you adopt to achieve those skills or understand that content?

   ii) What behaviours will you adopt to achieve those results?

   iii) How committed are you to following these strategies?

Approach

Use the steps below to implement change and move towards the destination of your choice (you may like to use your responses from the previous reflect questions). Use the core vision you wrote in chapter 2 (p. 110). Open your mind to infinite possibilities and dare to dream. Sync and balance your core vision to your dream and write a vision target. Use this specific vision to establish a targeted practice.

1. *Value*: What is your core vision.

2. *Vision*: What do you dream of doing? Be imaginative and think freely – remember this is a dream, it is not constrained by perceptions of reality.

3. *Sync*: Is your dream in harmony with your core vision?

4. *Target Vision*: What specific action can you take to make that dream come true? Set a SMART target.

   Specific

   Measureable

   Attainable

   Relevant

   Time bound

5. *Balance*: Monitor your thoughts and emotions toward your target – what do you think and how do you feel about your target? Are these thoughts and feelings helpful? Are you willing to be responsible for your actions?

6. *Build*: List the actions which will move you toward your target. You may like to write each one on a separate sticky note as this makes them easier to move around in the next step.

7. *Prioritise*: Organise your actions. What will you do:

Today?

Tomorrow?

By the end of the week?

By the end of the month?

8. *Commit*: Write a commitment statement and position it in a visible place. Decide to be disciplined.

I commit to_____I will be disciplined and achieve_____ by_____

9. *Execute*: Start today, take action and complete a task that will move you toward your target.

Have you committed to
a valued course
of purposeful action;
a planned approach
that moves resolutely
towards your intended target?

Chapter 4: The Audience

Consequence Awareness

Have you ever set a target and then felt awash by a *what if* flood? Sometimes, even when the projected target is something you really want, fear of what may happen threatens to overwhelm the enthusiasm you expected to feel. Before we explore possible strategies to manage these emotions, I would like to create a scenario. As you read, think about how you might respond in a similar situation.

> Imagine being given the opportunity to travel overseas on a school trip. You may feel excited and eagerly imagine what lies ahead. As you talk to your friends this anticipation grows and you ride high on a cloud of animated pleasure. At home you discuss plans with your parents and they support your desire to travel. Eagerly, they regale you with travel tales about eating unfamiliar food and experiencing different cultural traditions.

> BAM,
> despite good intentions, your parents have
> opened the *worry bird* cage.

> Yet your parents continue to speak. They plan travel insurance and visits to the doctor for possible vaccinations. They happily highlight all of the new encounters you are likely to have.

> The escaped worry birds land on your shoulders,
> and they are heavy.

> You begin to imagine all the things that may go wrong.

The *worry birds* start pecking your ear,
the *what if* flood gates have been opened.

That night you go to bed and fear of the unknown
battles against anticipation of discovery.

How will you proceed?

This is a moment of choice. This is the stage where you can allow emotions, acknowledge thoughts and then manage them. It is also the point where you may begin to write. Or to be more specific, you may begin to plan.

1. Build a mental picture of your destination.

2. Research to gain more knowledge about the destination.

3. Acknowledge possible consequences.

4. Sync and balance these possible consequences – determine if they represent an outcome you are willing to accept.

5. Isolate areas that are within your sphere of influence from those over which you have no control.

6. Identify strategies you can adopt to minimise or manage the outcomes you can control.

7. Make an informed choice – is this what you want?

8. Set a series of targets which reach toward the destination.

9. Write a plan – prioritise and align targets.

10. Commit to enthusiastic and persistent action.

This is a process that works best when it is written. Remember the worry birds do not exist in reality. They are a mental construct; a fear of a possible future occurrence. This is why writing is so useful. Writing moves thoughts and emotions from the ether to the page; a page you can read, with words you can control. It is this sense of control which may offer respite from the worry birds' twittering chatter.

When you take charge by identifying possible challenges and then proposing possible responses, you begin to 4C your future. Of course, it is important to be aware of consequences. It is necessary to recognise that sometimes, things go wrong. This is not a negative attitude; rather it is a realistic and responsible mindset. Being aware of consequence and choosing to manage the outcomes you have control over is not the same as worrying. A character may sit and worry, but an author recognises responsibility and takes action.

Remember, as you GRASP your way along the *Learning Path* you hold a *Master Key*. You have the techniques to manage outcomes and solve puzzles. This is the flexible approach; an approach where you are continually proposing, testing and re-proposing. In other words, a rite or quest where you are continually learning about learning.

Now
Breathe.
Breathe fully.
Breathe deeply.
Breathe purposefully.

Story: The Rite IV

'There it is!'

Now that she was *There*, it all seemed absurdly simple; the path didn't stretch outward, it reached inward! With a wry grin, and carefully measured step, Tania walked forwards. Beneath her feet she noticed that the soft earth of the forest had given way to the solid rock of the cave. As the light faded a rabble of butterflies rose in her tummy.

'Breathe,' she reminded herself.

Just breathe.
Full breaths.

She allowed herself time to adjust to the darkness of the cave – so still after the riotous tones of the forest. Her breathing became her focus as she waited for her mind to settle. The butterfly rabble became a gentle flutter and an energised excitement began its ascent through her body.

'It's time,' she thought. 'It's time for the final stage of the Warrior's Rite.'

Onward … inward she travelled. The darkness was absolute. However, the confronting fear Tania expected to feel was kept at bay – repelled by the reassuring sound of the rhythmic rise and fall of her own breath. Tania recognised this black void. It was the penultimate step of her quest. Instead of lamenting, she welcomed it.

'Why is black so feared?' she mused. 'Why is it regarded as a malevolent foe – an absence of colour reserved for emptiness?'

This inner space, this dark void, was alive with possibility. It was a place where the concept of a solitary right or wrong answer dissolved in the face of a million creative solutions. Tania became aware of the leisurely peace which rested comfortably alongside her growing excitement.

She knew the endless search was over, she did not need to question,
What if I can't decide which direction to take?
What if I make a mistake?
What if I make the wrong choice?
What if ...
What if ...

She knew she could trust herself and find the answer. Expectations disintegrated and in their absence was a place Tania's mind could rest. Here, in the folds of self-acceptance she had found the honour code of the warrior.

Onward and inward she travelled.
So close now.

The darkness gave way to a luminescent glow.

She was
There.

Tania's eyes opened wide in wondrous amazement as a sea of radiant shapes beckoned her closer. With awe laden steps she glided toward the glistening spirals – they pulsed with a life of their own. This was the fabled library of the inner scroll, the place at the centre of the *World of Expression*. It was the warrior's prize; their right. Here she would create with confidence, courage and compassion. Tania remembered the tools she had brought with her and intuitively grasped the next step.

It was time to write.

A table waited patiently in the middle of the chamber. Atop its polished surface was an unfurled scroll, a pot of shimmering liquid and a quill. Beside the table rested a chair. This ornately carved, softly cushioned haven was an anchorage point that promised comfort.

Tania settled into a relaxed position on the author's chair. Drawing on the training that had brought her this far, she began to record the scenes of her life. Words formed easily on the page. Tania recalled the wisdom of her grandmother and wrote with the resilient strength that was her legacy. Tania felt her father's optimism and love of life infuse the glittering ink. Her mother's kind consideration for others reminded her to give aid to those weaker than herself. Not to be forgotten, the observant persistence of her brothers aligned with the sometimes challenging, often comforting, advice offered by friends and teachers. Blended throughout was Tania's own inquisitive imagination.

She continued to write.

She reflected on her past, and observed the events which had led her to this stage. She recognised the robust root system which supported her; a legacy from family and friends. Tania observed all with fresh eyes.

Next, Tania reached beyond her personal history and into a vision of her future. She began to chronicle her dreams and laid a path for what was to come. She chose her direction and marked it with recognisable targets.

Time passed in simple silence. Eventually, Tania leaned back in her chair and took a moment to gaze around the room. Light flickered upon the cavernous walls reflecting the glow of a thousand coloured scrolls. *This is not the end*, she thought calmly. Tania knew there was so much more ahead. Glancing down at her own scroll, she felt an invigorated sense of calm. The environment may change. Seasons would revolve and the outer word would shift. Yet here, in this inner place of *Expression*, it was possible to see, to hear and to feel a sense of control. This was the *Present* – the reward for completing the warrior's Rite.

241

Taking a deep breath, Tania placed her scroll into one of the waiting recesses. She watched as the scroll assumed the same luminescent colours as the ones surrounding it. Within moments, her scroll thrummed in unison with the others sending out colourful rays of light. Satisfied, Tania readied herself for the path ahead. She smiled confidently and with shoulders set and chin raised, she placed one moccasined foot in front of the other.

<u>Step 9 on the *Learning Path*</u>

Take a breath
Breathe mindfully

<u>*Step 1*</u> *encouraged you to peer inside yourself and discover who you are.*

<u>*Step 2*</u> *asked you to 4C your future.*

<u>*Step 3*</u> *proposed the discovery of your own place.*

<u>*Step 4*</u> *offered the opportunity to uncover your* Honour Compass.

<u>*Step 5*</u> *invited you to recognise your emotions.*

<u>*Step 6*</u> *called upon you to process your feelings.*

<u>*Step 7*</u> *asked you to reflect upon your thoughts.*

<u>*Step 8*</u> *demonstrated targeted purpose.*

Now it is time for the ninth step.

*Will you breathe
the breath
of balance?*

Step 9: Take a Breath

Have you ever stood in front of an audience and felt as if butterflies were dancing across your heart; or perhaps ramming into your ribcage? These fluttering waves of excitement or wafted nervous programs may have left you gasping for breath.

Take a breath now.

Take a deep breath.

Take another.

A carefully measured,

Slowly released,

Deep breath.

As you breathe slow deep breaths, you may start to notice those butterflies settle. They gently alight, their wings fluttering in peaceful rhythm, a series of flickering filaments which inspire and energise. This is why we breathe. We inhale the elements necessary for life; we breathe to draw in oxygen.

Chapter 4: The Audience

Throughout *MyStory* you have been encouraged to explore your internal pathways and move toward a centred stage. As you stand upon your stage, looking toward the audience of yourself, you may feel a similar nervousness to the adrenaline-fuelled anxiety which simmers before delivering a speech in class. Can you remember the advice your teacher gave you to minimise these nerves?

- Plan carefully and research thoroughly – feel confident in your knowledge of the topic.
- Commit to regularly repeated practice – rehearse in front of a mirror or a friendly audience (such the family pet, or potted plant).
- Take a series of deep, full breaths before you commence.

Did you know this advice holds firm to settle the flutters you may feel when faced with your inner audience?

Remember, as the author of your *MyStory*, you are crafting the script of your life; and you are preparing it for you. In this sense, the context of *MyStory* is your life and the audience is you.

Musing Meditation

As anyone who has attended a first aid course knows, a patient who is not breathing is in danger; we need to breathe in order to survive. Yet, how often do you consciously think about the breaths you take?

Try this quick exercise:

Breathe in slowly. As you breathe in, actively think about the path the air takes as it moves into your body. Then, as you exhale, monitor the air as it leaves. As you continue to breathe, following the path of your breath, notice the area in your body that expands and contracts; is it the chest or the tummy? Recognise the length of your breath; is it complete – are your breaths shallow or deep?

You have just become consciously aware of breathing.

How does it feel
when you notice your breath?

If breathing is an essential component of life, it makes sense to suggest that focused breathing is a useful approach for a focused life. Actively tuning in to the process of breathing can help focus your awareness since it provides respite from that internal chatter which whips veraciously through the mind. Put simply, an awareness of the breath may offer a sense of calmness.

However, in a somewhat ironic twist, being actively aware of breathing can also be a brain training exercise. While being consciously calm, the unconscious may dance. This juxtaposed position is a playground for creativity and generating solutions. It can present a secure space from which to begin recognising what it feels like to be peaceful. Additionally, it can foster greater awareness of the relationship between the conscious and unconscious.

Chapter 4: The Audience

As an English teacher I have encouraged my students to become aware of their breathing before they write. Time and time again the students in my classes have experienced a sense of reassured inspiration as a result of a short *Musing Meditation* – the style of breathing exercise I like to use in the classroom. In essence it refers to a short relaxation exercise followed by a brief guided meditation where students are encouraged to become aware of their breathing and then visualise themselves being safely connected to the ground. From this secure position they may haze into a world of inner expression.

You may recall that a muse in Greek legend was a mythical being who inspired the creation of stories and music. As a verb, 'to muse' means to contemplate or reflect. This is why I like to describe classroom meditation as *Musing Meditations*. It is a style of meditation which builds awareness of inner expression and allows a student to explore their inner chambers.

One of the benefits of this meditation is its potential to suspend disbelief and unlock creativity. It can help a student develop a courageous mindset for doing rather than deliberating over how to do. I have found that attaining mastery over the dreaded unknown is possible when imagination reveals the confidence to explore possibility.

This courage can be found through flexibility and a willingness to be creative. In this space it is possible to transform mistakes into opportunities to learn. These are the times when it is possible to relax in the awareness of the process being as meaningful as the result and discover that creating something from nothing is deeply satisfying. Therefore, *Musing Meditation* can be a meaningful way to discover more about the connections between our internal and external worlds.

It is not my intention to offer a detailed explanation of meditation and its benefits here. Rather my objective is to introduce you to the concepts so that you may make a choice, and if you like, explore the practice further.

Meditation

Meditation, while holding a number of variant definitions, may be seen as a practice of focused awareness that moves towards a quiet mind and a relaxed contemplative state. Meditation may be thought of as introducing yourself to yourself and becoming more aware.

Meditation and the Successful Student

Meditation has the potential to increase your capacity to concentrate, retain more of what you learn and access your inner creativity. It achieves this by offering you an opportunity to develop a focused, relaxed state where you can centre and balance yourself. Over time, you will notice yourself becoming more aware of the manner in which your thoughts and emotions influence your beliefs and actions. As you become more aware of yourself and your surroundings, you are likely to feel calmer, more in control and more confident in your ability to respond to what lies ahead. At this point you may find yourself daring to dream. As you become more alert to inner expression, you may begin to hear the 'aha' revelations and see the flashes of insight which bring innovative solutions to over-deliberated problems.

Meditation to Relieve Stress

Meditation can help you identify and release 'trapped' anxiety – old thoughts, feelings and emotions that have been forced into hiding. Imagine a bottle of cola that has been shaken and left on the table. What will happen if you open it? It is likely to explode like a fountain, drenching you in dark ooze.

You can think of your unresolved thoughts, feeling and emotions as similarly trapped energy. One way to release this pressure is simply to breathe – breathe deeply, purposefully and consciously. Later, once you have relieved the pressure it is possible to re-examine the old thoughts, feelings and emotion. You may examine them dispassionately and recognise them for what they are.

In other words, once you have identified emotions, and allowed them rather than hiding them or avoiding them, you are in a position to face, address and learn from them. The key is to be present in the now rather than embedded in the past or locked in the future.

Meditation in Practice

Although there are many variations, basic meditation simply involves focused breathing. I suggest attending a meditation class, but you can also buy guided meditation tracks or Apps.

In most instances you will be asked to sit comfortably on the floor or in a chair with your back straight and feet on the ground. Then breathe deeply all the way in and all the way out, each time noticing the expansion as your tummy fills with air and the contraction as you exhale.

As you focus on your breathing you may notice thoughts intruding as worry birds and chattering monkeys clambering for attention. Simply let them have their say and gently dismiss them – let words float away without response. As you continue to focus on the breath, feeling it relax and soothe, these thoughts generally fade and you can simply notice the breath as it moves through your body.

Maintaining Focus

One technique that I find useful to clear my mind is to focus the breath on a particular part of my body. Put simply, I imagine breathing into my tummy, or heart, or even legs. In my mind I ask myself which part of my body needs to be revitalised, and I breathe into that place.

Story: My Muse

'Let the music fill the spaces in your head ... don't think ... just write.'

Huh ... Is she kidding ...?
Spaces ...?
What planet is Miss K on this time?

Ignoring the mournful sounds pulsing from soul-sucking speakers, John resolutely fixed his gaze on the world through the window. Desperately clutching to hold tumultuous thoughts, he searched for a weapon to banish the blanket of calm which threatened to settle across his shoulders. He found three: *Frustration, Resentment* and *Anger*. This trio were old friends. They lent him the strength to shrug off *Tranquillity*'s embrace, but it was the entrance of his old mentor *Analysis* that managed to exile any lingering sense of peace.

Analysis, that faithful guardian of possible options, deliberately initiated the infinite scenario program. This what if database implied answers. John settled into his search. Answers were the prize. Only they could offer relief. Answers were tangible, they were absolutes. They were real. However, it seemed that no matter how hard he searched or how many options he analysed, those answers remained elusive.

But they were out there.
John figured they were out there.
Just beyond sight.

The task at hand was writing a narrative. Exams were approaching so the future promised endless hours of revision. Miss K had been promoting relaxation techniques and pointing to current research which suggested listening to music with 60 beats per minute aided study. According to theory, this music encouraged the brain to enter a particular brain wave pattern that optimised learning. Miss K was attempting to demonstrate its value while also revising for the upcoming English exam by requiring the class to write a story using music as a stimulus. She said it was a task designed to maximise learning outcomes through meeting multiple learning styles; typical teacher rhetoric that simply translated in student speak to 'blah, blah, blah'.

Narrative writing had long been the bane of John's existence. It seemed futile, directionless and just plain dumb. It offered no tangible function, it did not answer a question, nor did it provide a solution. It simply frustrated him when he could not find the words to match the images within and, worse, tortured him by forcing him to expose his inner worlds. John hated the expectations. They appeared to be based on an assumption that he had a story to tell. Perhaps he did, but it wasn't one he was willing to share. It was his story and he was still figuring out where it was going and how it might end. Besides, other people may not like it and they were sure to use it against him. Worse still, it could become a standard by which they would judge him. So he resorted to supplying someone else's story; the story he believed they wanted to read.

What story did Miss K want this time? Which topic will generate the highest mark but require the least amount of effort? Is there a movie that I can adapt? What if nothing comes into my mind? What if I run out of time before I finish the story? What if I can't spell the words correctly? What if I don't use figurative language; shit, what is 'figurative language'?

The questions cascaded with military precision. They filled the spaces in John's head with crippling anxiety. 'But Miss K wanted the music to fill the spaces in my head.' The war began. John struggled. His heart wept. The music had failed.

I knew it! John felt a glimmer of satisfaction. I knew this was all crap designed to offer false hope. This listening to music is just a

251

theory designed by some guy to scam money out of gullible fools like Miss K.

John held tight to the rope offered by righteous indignation and began binding it around himself to anchor his thoughts. Although he chafed against the restricted movement, he felt secure within the coils and settled into the familiar space to ride out the battle.

The music continued. Soft sounds of content reached forward to swirl in unobtrusive waves gently dissolving the knots restricting his progress. John noticed his breathing fall into a regular pattern. Within minutes, he began following the path of his breath. He forgot to think. He felt. He noticed. He became aware. He made a choice. *Trust, Faith* and *Awareness* walked beside him. He started to write his story.

Centred and Balanced

It is possible to move beyond the *what if* scenarios that loop endlessly on a repeat cycle to a state of centred awareness. A person who meditates regularly is usually able to recognise patterns of brooding and move through to the other side of their concerns. In other words, rather than being locked in a cycle of worry about an unidentified threat in an unknown future that is yet to happen, they focus on the present, allowing thoughts and feelings as they watch them from a state of objective awareness. They become aware of the now. This is why I like to think of *Musing Meditation* as a key that unlocked my eyes.

I have always been a highly visual person. I take pleasure in the beauty around me. I love recognising shapes; watching a play of light; tracing clouds which cross the moon; following waves that nibble a headland. Yet I remember very clearly the day I *opened* my eyes. I had attended a number of meditation classes and was starting to notice the benefits of the relaxed state meditation offered. After the third class I was driving home and realised my ability to see had been enhanced. For the first time in my driving experiences I actually noticed what a traffic light looked like. I realised that the red circle was actually a series of smaller lights arranged in a circular shape; and it was beautiful. From that moment my perception of red lights changed. I reframed my vision and recognised that traffic lights were an opportunity to stop and reflect on the beauty around me, rather than feeling frustrated by something that was obscuring my path.

Becoming self-aware, setting targets and living purposefully may appear challenging, especially when everything seems to be in a state of flux. Yet if we can find balance we can find a stable stage and achieve harmony. I realise this may sound a lot like Mr Miyagi or Mr Han (depending on which version of *The Karate Kid* you have seen), but I find it interesting that the movie was re-made within the space of 26 years. Perhaps it highlights, or rather reinforces, the message that young people (and not-so-young people) are struggling to find a path of peaceful coexistence.

Have you ever felt as though you discovered
'the answer'
only to find circumstances had changed?

This is why meditation can be helpful; it offers an anchor, a sense of inner awareness which is particularly relevant during those times we feel as though we have been cast adrift. As you become more aware of yourself and your surroundings, you are likely to feel calmer, more in control and more confident in your ability to respond to what lies ahead.

Meditation can help you find balance ...

Approach

This is a very simple breathing exercise which I use to settle my mind before I sleep.

Lay comfortably on your back with your head on a pillow and close your eyes.

Take a deep breath, gently drawing the air into your lungs and slowly releasing it.

As you take in a second breath, feel any tension you may be holding in your feet.

As you release the breath imagine releasing any tension in your feet.

With your next breath in, feel any tension you may be holding in your calves.

As you release the breath imagine releasing any tension in your calves.

As you take in the next breath, feel any tension you may be holding in your quads.

As you release the breath imagine releasing any tension in your quads.

With your next breath in, feel any tension you may be holding in your stomach.

As you release the breath imagine releasing any tension in your stomach.

As you take in the next breath, feel any tension you may be holding in your chest.

As you release the breath imagine releasing any tension in your chest.

With your next breath in, feel any tension you may be holding across your shoulders.

As you release the breath imagine releasing any tension across your shoulders.

As you take in the next breath, feel any tension you may be holding around your eyes.

As you release the breath imagine releasing any tension around your eyes.

Take one more conscious breath, all the way in and then gently release it.

Although this exercise is very simple and very gentle, if you experience any discomfort, please stop and speak to a professional meditation teacher or counsellor. Remember meditation is not a substitute for professional treatment or advice. What I have described here is simply a relaxation exercise that I have found useful.

Breathe deeply as you
move along the Learning Path.

Be mindful,
Be purposeful,
Be present

and

Live the moments.

<u>Step 10 on the *Learning Path*</u>

Cultivate an aware mind.
Reading and writing critically

<u>*Step 1*</u> *encouraged you to peer inside yourself and discover who you are.*

<u>*Step 2*</u> *asked you to 4C your future.*

<u>*Step 3*</u> *proposed the discovery of your own place.*

<u>*Step 4*</u> *offered the opportunity to uncover your* Honour Compass.

<u>*Step 5*</u> *invited you to recognise your emotions.*

<u>*Step 6*</u> *called upon you to process your feelings.*

<u>*Step 7*</u> *asked you to reflect upon your thoughts.*

<u>*Step 8*</u> *demonstrated targeted purpose.*

<u>*Step 9*</u> *revealed the balanced breath.*

Now it is time for the tenth step.

*Are you ready to
read and write with
a critical mind?*

Step 10: Cultivate an Aware Mind

Living the moment by being simultaneously aware of both the internal and external flows that surround us is a choice; and it is not always an easy one. There is often so much 'busyness' in life – so much that needs to be done, so many places to be and people to see – that it is easy to be lured by thoughts, or swept away by emotions.

Have you ever felt like a juggler?
No sooner does one ball land in your hand
than you need to throw it back into the air
to catch the ball that follows closely behind it?

These are the times when remembering to breathe can help. The moment of pause supplies the space to realign, refocus and re-energise. The power to continue is derived both from the renewing elements taken in through the air and the subtle gap between thinking and not thinking. In this ephemeral void, it is possible to simply experience the moment. This distraction-free zone offers the opportunity to be aware. This is the mindful stage of the author. This is the centred position from which they may draw the resources and knowledge to make an informed choice about what and how to write.

Choosing to become the author requires accountability. It is a choice which demands commitment. Being the author involves persistent, determined and flexible effort. It thrives on a confident, courageous, creative and compassionate attitude, which is internally generated. But it yields results commensurate with the effort expended. Being the author is intensely liberating and manifestly empowering. However, as Peter Parker's uncle counselled in the movie *Spiderman,*

Is This *MyStory*

'With great power comes great responsibility.'

In taking control of your life, you also inherit considerable responsibility. This responsibility is managed by collecting, monitoring and allowing your emotions and thoughts; then syncing and balancing them through your Honour Compass; so you can choose the actions which will move you toward your targeted purpose.

Therefore, just as you use techniques to read and write the pages of your life, it is also important to adopt a mindful approach to the physical processes of reading, writing, speaking, listening and viewing. This critically evaluative approach to literacy supports the development of knowledge. And, as Sir Francis Bacon suggested,

knowledge is power.

The objective of the tenth step on the *Learning Path* is to gather the folds of critical literacy around you. Wear it like a cape, it can shelter and protect you. At the same time, critical literacy is a ticket, it is a master key which can open the door to a *World of Expression* and the *Library of Life*.

This mindful approach to

literacy

is the key to

a successful

MyStory.

Mindfulness

The term 'mindfulness' refers to a state of being which is completely present in the 'now'. It involves focusing on what is happening, rather than what has happened or what might happen. Importantly it also refers to allowing present experiences and feelings without assigning labels. In other words, mindfulness is a term which describes a process whereby feelings, thoughts and experiences are encountered, acknowledged and let go.

In much the same way, alertness involves being aware of the present, as well as being ready and willing to recognise opportunity. Similarly awareness implies being consciously attentive to the current situation and thus receptive to changes in your present reality.

To picture this concept you may like to imagine surfing on a beautiful clear morning. In a mindful state you will experience the majesty, freedom and power of the wave as you share in its energy. You can relax and enjoy being present in the moment because you know your awareness will alert you to any potential danger (such as another rider dropping in). Do you think your surfing experience would be as magical if you spent your time constantly looking over your shoulder, watching every other surfer in the water, deliberately missing waves in the fear that someone else may catch the same wave?

Being aware of your surroundings offers the opportunity to be fully present and appreciative of the now rather than wallowing in a sea of what if scenarios.

By this stage in your reading you probably realise how being mindful can illuminate the *Learning Path* to the internal world of expression. It may also be applied to the literal expressive world.

Literally Mindful

You may be wondering how mindfulness applies to literacy. I believe that being 'mindfully literate' is a stepping stone to being critically literate. Being mindfully literate implies being aware of your own use of language, as well being aware of how language is used on you. This awareness offers the space to appreciate the message. In a sense being mindful of language is like having a heightened awareness of the communication process. This sense of alertness creates opportunities because we are more able to recognise those Eureka! flashes.

Remember, *Is this MyStory* is an extended metaphor. The primary theme imbued within the pages has been to become internally aware and to, figuratively, write your *MyStory*. My aim was to help you develop the learning skills required to assume responsibility and directorship of your own life. My secondary message was to develop or GRASP critical literacy skills. These skills can help you access and process information. In other words,

to learn about how you learn.

Therefore, throughout *MyStory* the words on the page have encouraged you to explore your perception of yourself. The skills you have gathered are powerful since they can be used to read and evaluate your inner *World of Expression*. However, at the same time, you have also been building your critical literacy skills. These skills provide tools which can help you learn and adapt to external change. The confidence this brings encourages a courageous, creative and flexible mindset. In other words, critical literacy builds a mindset for doing, rather than waiting for someone else to do.

This is what I find inspiring about teaching English. Frequently I tell my classes English is the most important subject on the school curriculum. Reaching out over the collective groans and accusations of bias, I explain that the critical literacy skills you learn in English can be applied to almost every aspect of your life. During English classes you learn so much more than how to read and write. You also learn how to GRASP life, you learn to:

- Consider the actions of characters and the opinions of authors (both fiction and nonfiction).
- Run those ideas through your personal system programming and consider alternate perspectives.
- Consider the impact of environment.
- Recognise register (the interplay of audience, context and purpose) and ascertain its effect on meaning.
- Evaluate and make a judgement about what you are reading, hearing and viewing.
- Synthesise ideas and skills to create fresh ones of your own.

To be fair, I must acknowledge the importance numeracy and the logical problem-solving skills learnt in Maths and Science classes. Nevertheless, since communication is a fundamental aspect of relationships, and relationships are a core component of life, developing the ability to communicate effectively as well as being able to solve problems through evaluating words, images, sounds and gestures, are perhaps the most valuable skills you will learn at school.

You may like to think about it this way, knowledge is transferred through communication and communication occurs through the written word, the spoken word and gestures. This transferral is both internal and external. This is why I place such a high value on literacy. When you are critically literate you place yourself in a position of choice. You are able to listen, view, read and understand. You can use that understanding to build awareness (both internally and externally) and then you can use that awareness to make informed choices.

Critical literacy supports learning.

Learning supports self-reliance.

Self-reliance perpetuates confidence, courage, creativity and compassion.

Confidence, courage, creativity and compassion generates renewable internal energy.

Renewable energy sustains a purposeful *MyStory*.

A purposeful *MyStory* aligns internally and externally to nestle within life's library.

Will you choose
to read and write
speak, view and listen
mindfully?

Reading Mindfully

I like to define 'reading mindfully' as 'being aware of what I am reading'. This means directing my attention to what is on the page rather than mentally rubbernecking to check in with the worry birds or chattering monkeys of my self-talk. Another way to think of mindful reading is to imagine being immersed in the story or engaged with the text.

In his book *You Gotta Be the Book*, teacher Jeffery Wilhelm suggests that the engaged readers in his classes enjoy the process of reading most when they participate in the action and make predictions. When reading fiction, these students enthusiastically assume a place within the story. Sometimes they adopt the standpoint of the protagonist, other times a friend and, sometimes, they assume the identity of an outside observer[17]. In other words, these active readers enter a world of expression and in this imagined place, they experience variant aspects of life without fear or boundaries. Such is the magic of stories.

To experience powerful learning, reading should also be reflective. This is why mindful reading is so important. Mindful reading allows the reader to experience alternative outlooks and draw creative inference. From here it is possible to synthesise fresh perspectives. In essence, new ideas are formed and learning takes place. This occurs because the mindful reader consciously questions the words on the page and actively compares the ideas to situations and concepts within their experience. Metaphorically speaking, information is run through internal system programs and checked for relevance, usefulness and validity. The program may then be synced for improved system performance.

However, too many students (and adults) tell me they hate reading. They bemoan the acres of text which must be ploughed through

[17] Jeffery D. Wilhelm, *You Gotta Be the Book: Teaching Engaged and Reflective Reading with Adolescents,* Teachers College Press, New York, 1997, pp 56, 57

at a teacher's command. I can understand their angst; they feel forced to read and may not have a clear reason to read. Reading is easier, and more enjoyable, when there is a legitimate and personally acknowledged purpose for reading. This is why choice and reframing can be useful. Put simply:

The key to successful reading is
identifying a reason to read.

Essentially this is a task to be undertaken by the individual because it relates to the personal targets set. Nevertheless, I can offer three generic reasons to read:

i) to unlock creative expression

ii) to uncover potential, explore possibility and broaden perspective

iii) to practise evaluating data

Reading is an important activity. It has the power to transport the reader to hidden worlds, fascinating spaces and mysterious realms. Reading offers insights into the minds and hearts of others, proving fresh perspectives, inspiring ideas and soothing relief. This is why I read. I read to learn, to experience, to grow, to break free and simply to rest within the pages.

Why do you read?
What do you read?

Is what we read important? Yes, of course it is. Just as overindulging in junk food plays havoc with our digestive system, overindulging in junk reading material plays havoc with our mind. To be a little more specific, texts which wallow in hopelessness, tragedy and misfortune may actually be a de-motivating force rather than an inspiring one. A simple remedy, as is the case with food, is to read a balanced diet which includes fiction and nonfiction. Interestingly, in keeping with the food analogy, just as eating breakfast offers the body the energy boost it requires to start the day, committing to a morning ritual which involves reading stimulating material, is a powerful boost for the mind. Therefore, over breakfast I like to read development-type texts (be they personal or professional) or books about inspirational people and events. I find reading material that is positive, instructional and inspiring establishes a constructive mindset which energises my day and encourages creativity.

Remember, reading is a skill, so it is possible to improve reading ability through focused practice. When you have identified an internally inspired reason to read and your reading has a targeted purpose, the motivation to practise is also likely to increase. This practice can sharpen your skills. Think of the basketballer who repetitively shoots hoops. With each shot they adjust their stance and train their muscles so that on match day they can perform at their peak. You can adopt a similar position with your reading – read frequently and read a variety of genres (fiction and non-fiction) and text types (newspapers, journals, blogs, novels, biographies etc).

Reluctant readers may find comfort in audio books. Audio books provide an entertaining option for improving reading skills while offering an alternative access to stories. Modern technology has furnished an extensive choice of easily accessible audio options. Audio books are easily downloaded directly onto MP3 players. However, a useful strategy to improve reading skills is to both listen to the recording and follow the words by reading the book.

Of course, reading mindfully is a choice. It is a recognition of the value to be found within the page. Throughout history, the ability to read (and write) has been held in high esteem because the capacity to make sense of squiggly lines on a page facilitates access to knowledge. While it is true that stored knowledge is now more accessible (and can be listened to as much as read), it is not necessarily easier to make sense of the squiggly lines. In fact the almost limitless access to information and the ease with which ideas can be shared is both a blessing and a curse. The sheer volume of information readily available at the click of a key is astounding and it is growing at an ever increasing rate.

How often do you go to Google for answers and
expect to know in an instant?

However, critical reading or GRASPing knowledge involves more than receiving an instant answer. Critical evaluation occurs through appreciating the value of the question more than being given an instantaneous answer. This is why developing the capacity to read mindfully is an important step on the *Learning Path*. In order to make sense of the immense and exponentially growing information available on the web, it is necessary to ask the questions which unlock ideas; to look beyond the box to innovative wisdom.

Approach

Commit to following this mindful reading strategy for at least a week. Then choose if you would like to adopt the practice as a regular ritual.

Discover   Borrow a motivational book from the library.

i) Read 3 – 4 pages each morning (while you eat breakfast). Read slowly and mindfully.

ii) While you shower (or while you travel to school), reflect upon the pages you read. GRASP the ideas transmitted through the content and consider how applicable they are to your life.

Writing Mindfully

The processes of reading and writing are closely linked, therefore it should come as no surprise that writing mindfully also implies being aware of expression. When I ask students to be mindful of expression, I ask them to focus on the task at hand so that they may write coherently and cohesively. At a purely mechanical level, mindful writing can develop and improve writing skills. This occurs because, as a writer focuses on choosing words and the way they are arranged into a sentence, while also monitoring how those sentences are built into paragraphs, they are attending to language techniques, spelling and punctuation.

However, as useful as it is to pay attention to these details, mindful drafting and editing offer an even greater opportunity to improve writing skills. The process of editing requires a person to re-read what they have written to check for accuracy and clarity. In essence, the writer mindfully reads their own work. As a result of this self-correction the writer is training themself to recognise how to write effectively. You may like to think of this as mindful literacy since it requires being simultaneously aware of the message and the processes being used to convey the message.

Remember, like reading, writing is a skill. Therefore you can improve your writing by writing frequently. Just as a golfer improves their accuracy at the pin through endless hours of training, and a musician improves the quality of their music through regular, disciplined practice, you can improve your ability to express yourself through the written word by writing regularly.

Writing mindfully offers more than simply improved writing skills. Whereas reading mindfully offers access to knowledge, writing mindfully helps to process it. The physical action of shaping words takes time, moving a pen or pencil across a page is usually slower than the creation of thoughts which are seeking substance. As a result, writing offers the opportunity to be mindfully aware of what is being written. This can help a writer focus on the task at hand. It can help them distinguish their thoughts and recognise their emotional responses. Of course, it is also possible to type mindfully, however in a digital age where touch typing contributes to speedy recording, the choice to type mindfully is a conscious one.

Similarly, since writing gives form to feelings and thoughts, the process of transferring the electrical impulses of the brain into a tangible entity provides an opportunity to actually see and physically manipulate ideas. In this way it is possible to consider thoughts and emotions from a more objective, dispassionate stance. One writing context which is particularly useful for processing thoughts is journaling.

Journaling

Frequently when emotions or thoughts run wild and unchecked they can build into ghost particles which are difficult to manage. However, by capturing them in print, you can gain a measure of control. With a sense of control comes the understanding that you have a choice. You can choose what to write next, so you can choose a response.

> *Can you recall times when it was difficult to*
> *define your thoughts or*
> *explain how you felt?*

Often the process of writing, or journaling, can help. By giving physical form to thoughts and emotions, journaling can help you move through your thoughts and emotions to a place where you can see them for what they are. In this form they may be viewed from different perspectives and when necessary, stored, thrown away, shared, or simply sent into the ether.

For this reason the practice of journaling can be extremely useful especially when an emotion or thought causes dis-ease, dis-comfort, frustration or even guilt. At these times it may be useful to write what flows through your mind. Write until you can actually see what is underneath. If you look honestly at those emotions and thoughts, you may see an alternative perspective. From here, an innovative solution may present itself.

The movie *Freedom Writers* demonstrates how powerful the process of mindful writing can be. It portrays a real life situation where journal writing gave students a voice; journaling gave these students an opportunity to reflect upon their thoughts and feelings. Teacher Erin Gruwell told her students:

> *Everyone has their own story.*
> *It is important for you*
> *to tell your own story.*

As you have no doubt recognised, this advice is very similar to the concept underpinning *MyStory*. You may like to watch this film. See for yourself what may be achieved by taking responsibility for your actions through writing your *MyStory*. Remember, this film is based on a true story.

Approach

Have you been adding to your journal? Now it is time to start a second journal. Your first journal provided an opportunity to reflect, the second one offers a chance to clear.

Clear: **A Clearing Approach**

Write regularly in a specially designated Clearing Notebook. For the first week, make an entry each night. Use this time to clear any unwanted thoughts. Write them on the page and leave them there. This is an opportunity to vent and release before sleeping. *Do not* read over past entries. This is a place to write through your thoughts and feelings, rather than a place to reflect.

Create: **A Musing Approach**

Keep writing weekly entries in your journal or blog. This is where you may like to reflect on your thoughts and feelings and explore your perceptions. Write about whatever you feel comfortable writing about. Re-read some of your earlier entries, have any of your perceptions changed?

Speaking, Listening and Viewing Mindfully

I understand that not everyone enjoys reading. I accept that for some people, writing is not an enjoyable pastime. However, I hope that this book has inspired you to enter the *World of Expression*. This is a world which accepts everyone. Anyone with the will to enter, the resolve to accept self-responsibility and the determination to take action, has the capacity to

> *open the door,*
> *be aware of their surroundings,*
> *ask questions, and*
> *discover fresh perspectives.*

> *This is the Rite of the Author.*

> *It is*

> *the Learning Path.*

Remember, literacy involves so much more than reading and writing. Although traditional understanding of the term described a person's ability to read and write, in a modern world that definition has been extended to include most forms of communication. This is why, in addition to reading and writing, your English classes probably include units of work that focus on the skills of speaking, listening, viewing and representing. It is possible to extend the definition of literacy even further to include emotional literacy (being able to read emotions and thoughts), digital literacy and even financial literacy. However, for now, I would simply like to remind you that it is possible to speak, listen and view from a mindfully literate point of view.

To a large extent I have already hinted at the importance of these skills. For example, I suggested that it is important to

Is This *MyStory*

be aware of your self-talk

and

say it the way you want it.

I have also referred to films to illustrate particular ideas and concepts. Do you know why?

Before answering that question, take a step back. Do you remember what I wrote in the opening pages of *MyStory*? I expressed my belief that stories have facilitated the transmission of traditions, histories and belief systems. Stories may be fictional, biographical or even historical, but in every case they have the power to transport the audience to other realms. In other words, they allow audiences to participate remotely in the lives of others.

Why do you think I have chosen to use the word 'audience' instead of 'reader'? I have used audience, because stories may be viewed and heard as well as being read. We watch films, we listen to people's conversations – we see and hear other people's stories. This is why, in addition to novels, I used movies to demonstrate the practical applications of particular ideas. Films (as well as documentaries, podcasts and conversations) offer the opportunity to experience stories.

Therefore, just as it is important to read and write mindfully, it is also important to speak, listen and view mindfully. In essence, the skills required are the same. Being mindful of your visual and audio expression involves GRASPing content, both the content you deliver and the content you receive.

So, the next time you view a movie or watch a favourite television program, you may like to watch it mindfully and then consciously talk about it.

Gather information which is relevant to your target.

Reflect on the ideas and determine if it is useful, truthful or aligned with your core values.

Analyse concepts for evidence of bias, consider credibility and recognise register.

Synthesise the ideas presented with your *Honour Compass* and your experience.

Propose alternate viewpoints or opinions.

To place this in a practical context I would like to share one of our family rituals. I believe that just as mindful reading and writing offers the opportunity to share imaginative experiences, mindful viewing, listening and speaking can open the door to creative expression. Therefore, ever since my children were young, we have enjoyed watching their favourite television programs together (my daughter and I share an enjoyment of science fiction and fantasy; my son and I enjoy investigative programs). We watch these shows attentively and then discuss the lives and actions of the characters.

Therefore, even if you do not like to read, even if you do not love to write, you can be mindfully literate. It is your right. You can be aware of how words are used to communicate (be they in written or audio form), how images convey meaning and how gestures and facial expressions express thoughts and feelings.

This awareness of your role
within the communication process
places you in the author's position.

Mindful
reading, writing,
speaking, viewing and listening
opens the door to the
World of Expression.

With this door literally and figuratively opened,
the skills and knowledge required
to become the author
are within easy reach.

Story: The Key II

Liz and John stood for a moment in respectful silence before gleefully turning to each other. Both spoke at once.

'Awesome.'

'Amazing.'

'So humongous.'

'So beautiful.'

'I love this place.'

'Thanks for encouraging me.'

John smiled and gave Liz a playful hug. 'Aw … you know I'd never let you give up. How could I? It's like you're part of me.'

Liz grinned and dropped under his arm to dance out of reach. 'Yep, but there's no need to get sentimental about it.'

'Geez girl, watch who you're calling sentimental, you may ruin my—' John didn't finish his sentence. His gaze had been captured by a single figure seated in the distance.

Following his line of sight, Liz gasped in amazement. 'Who do you think she is?'

Hunched over a table was a girl dressed in primitive skins. Her feet were covered by rough moccasins and at her side was a crude bow, an ornately carved spear and a travel-worn knapsack. Occasionally she raised a slender arm to absently brush at a strand of dark hair which had escaped from a loose clasp at the nape of her neck. It was clear that she was utterly focused on her task.

John cupped his hand to his mouth in readiness to call a greeting to the strange warrior girl, but paused as a gentle pressure was placed on his arm.

'She won't … Look …'

John followed Liz's outstretched finger. A dazzling mass of colour swarmed around the girl and it was obvious that the glistening kaleidoscope would soon obscure her from view. When the luminescent force settled, the girl had gone. In her place were the spiralling shapes Liz and John first noticed when they stood upon the stage.

'You saw …We both saw that right. You saw her didn't you? She was there … right there.' John's faltering voice reflected his attempt to make sense of what he had seen.

'Yeah … a girl was sitting there, colourful lights came, and now she's gone … I wonder what she was d—' Liz stepped toward the place the girl had left behind.

'Hang on, it might not be sa—' John's words fell into empty space.

Liz glanced back over her shoulder. She paused, then smiled. 'Remember what you said up there? We do or we don't do, we go on, or we turn back … we don't just stand here, we act. Aren't you even the least bit curious?'

'Course, but just be aware of where you are going.' John settled his hand into hers and together they stepped forward.

Bright spirals glowed around them. Curious cylindrical shapes vibrated with electrical force thrumming in rhythmic sequence. Awestruck, the pair watched as an aurora took shape.

'Look,' Liz's voice was heavy with wonder, 'they're like cables or giant wires wrapping around …'

Chapter 4: The Audience

John's attention was focused elsewhere. 'This is like … hey … do you think it's some kind of massive circuit board? Is this … maybe it's a power grid?'

Shadowy images began to form. Filament shapes and gritty silhouettes slowly hazed into bold outlines. Faces appeared, bodies grew and a cornucopia of images unravelled.

Stories.
Life stories.

It was like watching a thousand movies, simultaneously being participants and observers.

Liz gasped, 'There she is. That girl. Is this her story? … Look at all …' Liz looked at John. 'Where are we? What is this place?'

'I don't know,' John answered slowly. 'It's like being in a giant computer, or inside some kind of collective mind, or maybe it is just one mind – one mind with many stories and hundreds of options.'

'Do you think ours is here?' Liz questioned softly.

John's answer was unwavering. 'Not yet. But just like she did, that warrior girl, we can write our story and add it *there*.'

A table waited patiently in the middle of the chamber. Atop its polished surface was an unfurled scroll, a pot of shimmering liquid and a quill. Beside the table rested a chair. This ornately carved, softly cushioned haven was an anchorage point that promised comfort ...

Will you,
Use the Key to
Open the Door
to 4C your future,
and GRASP each moment?

Will you stand upon a centred Stage,
LEAF through life's pages
Face your Audience
Place your feet on the Target rungs
and focus on your Destination?

Will you
Write your
MyStory?

Conclusion

Now it is in your hands. Will you 4C your future? Do you have a vision, a purpose, a place to move toward, both literally and figuratively?

My role as your teacher was not to offer you answers, but rather to provide support while you developed the strength to ask your own questions and then uncover the answers for yourself.

This is the Learning Path.

You have been handed a *Key*, but you need to *Open the Door* and *Walk the Path*. I have given you a *Map*, but you need to locate yourself on it. You can choose where you want to go and you can actively plot your course. It is up to you to commit to following the route you have planned. Only you can take the steps that will lead you to achieve your purpose.

Remember *MyStory* is only a metaphor. It works by simplifying a complex process:

that of

moving from a character's attitude
to the author's mindset.

Have you ever heard the saying, 'the map is not the territory'? In other words, a map is a flat, one-dimensional representation of reality. Therefore, it is not possible to arrive at your destination simply by tracing your finger along a path on a piece of paper. To reach your destination, you need to go outside and literally walk an actual path. As you walk you will notice that life is multidimensional. It is not a flat line. In life you will encounter obstacles that need to be overcome and barriers that need to be surmounted. At these times you will need to draw upon your inner resources to maintain faith and continue toward your destination.

There will be times when mistakes are made; there will be times when things go wrong with no obvious actions and for no apparent reason. These testing times are aspects of living.

Are you ready to accept the challenge?
To learn what you can from
the experience and keep going?

Leave the past in the past and
enjoy the gift of the present.

Remember you can draw strength from your resource generator. That is why locating it and fortifying it is your *Rite*. From this mighty source you can access a valuable renewable energy. From this potent place you can draw the confidence, courage, compassion and creativity that underpins flexibility. You can learn new skills, adapt and remain in sync with your environment.

GRASP your future.
Accept the *Author's Rite*.
Write your *MyStory*.

Chapter 4: The Audience

Finally, I would like to share with you something my children shared with me. Putting ear buds into my ears my son said,

'Mum, you should listen to these lyrics, they're so true.'

My best friend gave me the best advice.
He said each day's a gift and not a given right.
Leave no stone unturned, leave your fears behind
And try to take the path less travelled by.
That first step is the longest stride

('If Today Was Your Last Day' – Nickleback)

As a mother I felt extremely proud. I realised that my son, a student who detested the study of English, was actually applying the skills of language to his life. He acknowledged the poetry within the lyrics of a song and he recognised how the subtle combination of words and harmonious melody inspired inner chords. He demonstrated critical awareness and used literacy mindfully.

Hearing this exchange my daughter directed me to a different song. Fresh ear buds were placed in my ears as she said,

'Mum, this is what I believe.'

I believe I can,
I believe I will,
I believe I know my dreams are real.
I believe I'll stand,
I believe I'll dance,
I believe I'll grow real soon,
That is what I do believe.

('I Believe' – Yolanda Adams)

285

Again I was extremely proud. My daughter (who incidentally does enjoy the study of English) had also recognised the powerful tools contained within stories. She synthesised the story's theme with the song's message and balanced her position upon a centred stage.

Always remember you have a choice. You can choose to be the author of your life, rather than being a character in someone else's.

Liz and John strode on to the *Learning Path*.
They took the *Key*, opened the *Door*
and placed their first step.
They were willing
to believe.

Tania accepted her birthright.
She travelled the *Learning Path*.
She found the Centre.
She fulfilled the
Warrior's
Rite.

How willing are you to take that first step.
Will you leave your fears behind?
Will you dare to dream?
Will you stride along
the *Learning Path*.
Will you write
MyStory?

**Welcome to a
World of Expression.**

Afterword

Do you feel inspired to put pen to paper (or finger to keyboard) and actually write your own *MyStory*?

Visit www.isthismystory.com now and read the responses written by other young people who are writing their *MyStory*.

A list of movies mentioned in *Is This MyStory*? that you may like to watch

☐ *Mary Poppins*

☐ *Dead Poets Society*

☐ *X-Men: First Class*

☐ *Bagger Vance*

☐ *The Empire Strikes Back*

☐ *Avatar*

☐ *A Knight's Tale*

☐ *Never Back Down*

☐ *Dangerous Minds*

☐ *Remember the Titans*

☐ *We Are Marshall*

☐ *Take the Lead*

☐ *Spiderman*

☐ *The Karate Kid*

☐ *Freedom Writers*

A list of plays mentioned in *Is This MyStory*? that you may like to watch or read

☐ *Romeo and Juliet*, William Shakespeare

A list of books mentioned in *Is This MyStory*? that you may like to read

Fiction

☐ *Looking for Alibrandi*, Melina Marchetta, (1992) Penguin Books, Australia

☐ *Tomorrow When the War Began,* John Marsden, (1993) Pan MacMillan Publishers, Australia

☐ *Lord of the Flies*, William Golding, (2003) Penguin, USA

☐ *The Alchemist*, Paulo Coelho (1998) HarperCollins Publishers, New York

☐ *To Kill a Mockingbird*, Harper Lee, (1997) Arrow Books, London

☐ *Who Moved My Cheese?*, Dr Spencer Johnson, (1999) Vermilion, London

☐ *Dracula*, Bram Stoker (2003) Penguin Classics

Non fiction

☐ *The 7 Habits of Highly Effective People*, Stephen Covey, (1995), Business Library, Melbourne

☐ *Biology of Belief*, Bruce Lipton, (2010) Hay House Australia

☐ *The Happiness Trap* Dr Russ Harris, (2007), Exisle Publishing Australia

☐ *Eat Pray Love*, Elizabeth Gilbert, (2007) Bloomsbury Publishing, London

☐ *Think and Grow Rich*, Napoleon Hill, *www.ThinkAndGrowRichGifts.com.au*

☐ *You Gotta Be the Book: Teaching Engaged and Reflective Reading with Adolescents*, Jeffrey Wilhelm, (1997), Teachers College Press, New York.

Web Pages

The Official Website of Stephenie Meyer, www.stepheniemeyer.com/bio.html

William Glasser Institute, www.wglasser.com

www.ingramcontent.com/pod-product-compliance
Lightning Source LLC
Chambersburg PA
CBHW060250100426
42742CB00011B/1705